W9-CIJ-446

Daily
Skill-Builders

Vocabulary

Grades 4–5

Writer
Vanessa Hession

Editorial Director
Susan A. Blair

Project Manager
Erica L. Varney

Cover Designer
Roman Laszok

Interior Designer
Mark Sayer

Production Editor
Maggie Jones

WALCH PUBLISHING

The classroom teacher may reproduce materials in this book for classroom use only.

The reproduction of any part for an entire school or school system is strictly prohibited.

No part of this publication may be transmitted, stored, or recorded in any form

without written permission from the publisher.

1   2   3   4   5   6   7   8   9   10

ISBN 0-8251-4780-8

Copyright © 2004

Walch Publishing

P. O. Box 658 • Portland, Maine 04104-0658

walch.com

Printed in the United States of America

Table of Contents

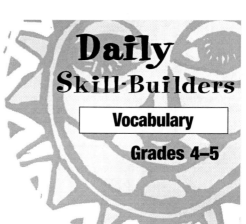

Daily Skill-Builders

Vocabulary

Grades 4–5

To the Teacher

Introduction to *Daily Skill-Builders*

The *Daily Skill-Builders* series began as an expansion of our popular *Daily Warm-Ups* series for grades 5–adult. Word spread, and eventually elementary teachers were asking for something similar. Just as *Daily Warm-Ups* do, *Daily Skill-Builders* turn extra classroom minutes into valuable learning time. Not only do these activities reinforce necessary skills for elementary students, they also make skill-drilling an engaging and informative process. Each book in this series contains 180 reproducible activities—one for each day of the school year!

How to Use *Daily Skill-Builders*

Daily Skill-Builders are easy to use—simply photocopy the day's activity and distribute it. Each page is designed to take approximately ten to fifteen minutes. Many teachers choose to use them in the morning when students are arriving at school or in the afternoon before students leave for the day. They are also a great way to switch gears from one subject to another. No matter how you choose to use them, extra classroom minutes will never go unused again.

Building Skills for All Students

The *Daily Skill-Builders* activities give you great flexibility. The activities can be used effectively in a variety of ways to help all your students develop important skills, regardless of their level.

Depending on the needs of your students and your curriculum goals, you may want the entire class to do the same skill-builder, or you may select specific activities for different students. There are several activities for each topic covered in *Daily Skill-Builders,* so you can decide which and how many activities to use to help students to master a particular skill.

If a student does not complete an activity in the allotted time, he or she may complete it as homework, or you may allow more time the next day to finish. If a student completes a skill-builder early, you may want to assign another. *Daily Skill-Builders* give you options that work for you.

Students in one grade level vary in their abilities, so each *Daily Skill-Builders* covers two grades. In a fourth-grade class, for example, some students may need the books for grades 3–4. Other students may need the greater challenge presented in the 4–5 books. Since all the books look virtually the same and many of the activities are similar, the students need not know that they are working at different levels.

No matter how you choose to use them, *Daily Skill-Builders* will enhance your teaching. They are easy for you to use, and your students will approach them positively as they practice needed skills.

School Action

These words are all **verbs,** or action words, used to describe things done at school. Read the verbs in the box below. Then fill in each line with the word from the box that best completes the sentence.

---

correct (*v.*) —to fix or make free from errors or mistakes

define (*v.*)—to find out and explain the meaning

outline (*v.*)—to make or prepare a summary of a subject

research (*v.*)—to study and investigate in order to discover and explain new knowledge

study (*v.*)—to use the mind to learn about something by reading, memorizing, or investigating

---

1. Before Jenny can write a paper about ancient Egypt, she must _____ the topic.

2. I do not know the meaning of that word. Can you _____ it for me?

3. Tonight the class will have to _____. We are having a big test tomorrow.

4. Our teacher lets us swap papers and _____ each other's work.

5. I _____ each day's reading. It helps me remember the main ideas.

Tools for Learning

Nouns are words that name people, places, objects, or ideas. Each noun in the box names a tool that people use to find information.

> atlas (*n.*)—a book of maps
> dictionary (*n.*)—a book that gives the meaning and pronunciation of
> words in alphabetical order
> encyclopedia (*n.*)—a book or set of books with all sorts of information
> in articles arranged alphabetically by subject
> Internet (*n.*)—a communications system that connects groups of
> computers all over the world
> questions (*n.*)—phrases or things asked in order to find information or
> answers

Dan needs to find the following information. He needs help! List the tools from the box that he can use. For some information, more than one tool can help.

1. how to find the capital of Montana _____

_____

2. what the word *metropolis* means _____

_____

3. how to contact people across the globe _____

_____

4. how to learn how a car engine works _____

_____

5. how to find the location of the Appalachian Trail _____

_____

School Words

School Sentences

Write a sentence using each word pair.

1. study/test_____

_____

2. define/understand_____

_____

3. outline/information _____

_____

4. correct/improve _____

_____

5. research/curious _____

_____

6. dictionary/help _____

_____

7. atlas/travel _____

_____

8. encyclopedia/many _____

_____

9. Internet/search _____

_____

10. questions/wise _____

_____

School Match

Below are vocabulary words and definitions. Find the definition of each vocabulary word. Write the letter of the correct definition on the line.

1. _____ study

a. a book of maps

2. _____ define

b. to list the main points or parts of

3. _____ outline

c. to use the mind to learn about something

4. _____ correct

d. a communications system that connects groups of computers all over the world

5. _____ research

e. to find out and explain the meaning of

6. _____ dictionary

f. something asked to find information or answers

7. _____ atlas

g. to fix or make free from mistakes

8. _____ encyclopedia

h. a book that gives the meaning and pronunciation of words in alphabetical order

9. _____ Internet

i. to study and investigate in order to discover and explain new knowledge

10. _____ questions

j. a book or set of books with information in articles arranged alphabetically by subject

School Words

People at School

We think of people who work at school as teachers. There are other people who have important jobs at school, too. Read the words in the box below. Then write a sentence about each school worker listed.

counselor (*n.*)—a person who gives advice
janitor (*n.*)—a person who cleans and takes care of a building
principal (*n.*)—the head of a school
secretary (*n.*)—a person who works in a school office and who handles records, letters, and other office work
volunteer (*n.*)—a person who gives or offers help or services without being paid

1. counselor _____

_____

2. janitor _____

_____

3. principal _____

_____

4. secretary _____

_____

5. volunteer _____

_____

School Spaces

A school building is made up of many different rooms and spaces, like your home. Here are some of those spaces. Read the nouns in the box below. Then describe how each space looks at your school. Use clear details!

> auditorium (*n.*)—a very large room or hall used for public gatherings or performances
>
> classroom (*n.*)—a room in a school or college where classes meet
>
> hallway (*n.*)—a corridor or pathway that connects rooms in a building
>
> library (*n.*)—a place where books or reference materials are kept for use but not for sale
>
> office (*n.*)—a place where business is done or a service is supplied

1. auditorium _____

_____

2. classroom _____

_____

3. hallway _____

_____

4. library _____

_____

5. office _____

_____

Schoolwork

Write the definition of each vocabulary word. Then circle each vocabulary word in the word search. Words appear across, down, or diagonally.

1. principal _____
2. library _____

3. secretary _____
4. classroom _____

5. counselor _____
6. auditorium _____

7. janitor _____
8. office _____

9. volunteer _____
10. hallway _____

```
P V A L V I T E E C V E L E V
H P R I N C I P A L O U L O O
A V O T E Q U C T A F M O C L
L T O P E L D A J S F S H Y U
S O F F U L T V I S T V A R N
H E H E V J O U E R E E L S T
E L C K O A S M S O N C L O E
L P O R S N L P I O R P W I E
V O E L E I U M S M S P A C R
A S E H O T L I B R A R Y E O
P Y C H N O A O B O U M S J F
F O P U F R S R C F Y H P E F
P E E R L E Y S Y J P A V C I
C O U N S E L O R I C E E K C
S A U D I T O R I U M M U O E
```

School Similes

A **simile** explains something by comparing it to something else. A simile always has the word *like* or *as*.

Example: Joe is **as** tall **as** a telephone pole.

Joe is not really as tall as a telephone pole. By comparing him to a pole, though, we get the idea that Joe is very tall.

Write a simile using each vocabulary word below.

1. principal _____

2. secretary _____

3. counselor _____

4. janitor _____

5. volunteer _____

6. library _____

7. classroom _____

8. auditorium _____

9. office _____

10. hallway _____

Daily Skill-Builders Vocabulary 4–5
walch.com © 2004 Walch Publishing

People and Places at School

Lots to Learn

There is so much to learn in life and so much information to study at school. To make things easier, information can be divided into areas of study. Here are the names of some of them. Read the words in the box below. Then list three terms related to each vocabulary word. One example has been done for you.

geography (*n.*)—a study of the location of living and nonliving
        things and the way they affect one another
history (*n.*)—a branch of knowledge that records and explains
        past events
mathematics (*n.*)—a study that explains numbers, amounts,
        measurements, and their relationships
science (*n.*)—a study that is concerned with collecting facts
        and forming laws to explain them
subject (*n.*)—a course of study

1. geography   north _____   _____   _____

2. history   _____   _____   _____

3. mathematics   _____   _____   _____

4. science   _____   _____   _____

5. subject   _____   _____   _____

Lots More to Learn

Read the names of more subjects in the box below. Then fill in each line with the word from the box that best completes the sentence.

anatomy (*n.*)—a science that has to do with the structure of the body
astronomy (*n.*)—the science of stars, planets, and other space objects and their motions
biology (*n.*)—a science that deals with living things and their relationships and behaviors
chemistry (*n.*)—a science that deals with the properties of substances and their changes
geology (*n.*)—a science of the history of Earth and its life, especially as recorded in rocks

1. The students studying _____ took a field trip to see the rock formations.

2. In order to become a surgeon and operate on people, one of the most important subjects is _____.

3. I am reading about _____ because I want to travel in space someday.

4. We wear safety glasses in _____ because we work with dangerous substances.

5. In _____, we learned how plants make energy.

Learning Words

Space for Rent

Read each definition. In the spaces, write the letters of the correct vocabulary word from the box.

anatomy	biology	geography	history	science
astronomy	chemistry	geology	mathematics	subject

1. a study that is concerned with collecting facts and forming laws to explain them

   _ _ _ _ _ _ _

2. the science of stars, planets, and other space objects

   _ _ _ _ _ _ _ _ _

3. a science that deals with living things and their relationships and behaviors

   _ _ _ _ _ _ _

4. a study of the location of living and nonliving things on Earth

   _ _ _ _ _ _ _ _ _

5. a course of study

   _ _ _ _ _ _ _

6. a science that deals with the properties of substances and their changes

   _ _ _ _ _ _ _ _ _

7. a study that explains numbers, amounts, and measurements

   _ _ _ _ _ _ _ _ _ _ _

8. a science of the history of the earth and its life, as recorded in rocks

   _ _ _ _ _ _ _

9. a science that has to do with the structure of the body

   _ _ _ _ _ _ _

10. a branch of knowledge that records and explains past events

    _ _ _ _ _ _ _

A Letter Home

Imagine that you are at a school camp. You study subjects in depth there. Write a letter home about the camp. Use at least five words from the box.

anatomy	biology	geography	history	science
astronomy	chemistry	geology	mathematics	subject

Dear _____,

_____

_____

_____

_____

_____

_____

_____

_____

_____

_____

_____

_____

Love,

_____

Learning Words

Tools of the Trade

These nouns all have to do with writing sentences. Read the nouns in the box below. Then follow the directions for each item.

adverb (*n.*)—a word used to describe a verb, an adjective, or another adverb

capital (*n.*)—the larger of the two types of written letters; uppercase

comma (*n.*)—a punctuation mark used to separate words or clauses in a sentence

period (*n.*)—a punctuation mark used to mark the end of a sentence or an abbreviation

pronoun (*n.*)—a word used in place of a noun

1. Circle the periods in these sentences. Then write a sentence of your own using a period.

   _____

2. Circle the comma in this sentence, and then write a sentence with a comma in it.

   _____

3. Circle the capital letters in these sentences. Then write a sentence using capital letters.

   _____

4. Circle the adverb in this sentence quickly, and then write a sentence with an adverb in it.

   _____

5. If you can find pronouns in these sentences, then circle them. Then write your own sentence with a pronoun in it.

   _____

Daily Skill-Builders Vocabulary 4–5
walch.com © 2004 Walch Publishing

Write Away!

People write every day—not just for school, but for other purposes, too. We make lists and write notes. We send e-mails and write letters to friends.

These nouns describe types of writing people do every day. Read the nouns in the box below. Then fill in each line with the word from the box that best completes the sentence.

> **application** (*n.*)—a form used to request something, often for information or a job
>
> **composition** (*n.*)—a short piece of writing done as a school exercise
>
> **form** (*n.*)—a printed sheet with spaces to write information
>
> **paragraph** (*n.*)—a block of writing made up of one or more sentences that has to do with one topic or idea or gives the words of one speaker
>
> **sentence** (*n.*)—a group of words with a subject and verb that tells a complete thought

1. I filled out a separate _____ for each job in which I was interested.

2. The new teacher asked us to write a(n) _____ for English class.

3. Please answer each question with a complete _____.

4. Henry had to fill out a long _____ at the hospital when he broke his leg.

5. Make sure that each _____ in your essay has a topic sentence.

In Your Own Words

In your own words, write the definition of each vocabulary word.

1. period _____

2. comma _____

3. capital _____

4. adverb _____

5. pronoun _____

6. form_____

7. sentence _____

8. paragraph _____

9. composition _____

10. application _____

Grammar and Writing Words

Caution: Words Crossing!

Match each clue with a vocabulary word from the box. Write the vocabulary word in the puzzle.

paragraph
form
composition
application
capital
comma
pronoun
sentence
adverb
period

Across

2. a punctuation mark to separate words or clauses

4. a word used in place of a noun

5. a punctuation mark used to mark the end of a sentence or an abbreviation

6. a form used to request something, often a job

9. writing made up of one or more sentences with one main idea

Down

1. a short piece of writing done as a school exercise

2. uppercase

3. a group of words with a subject and verb that tells a complete thought

7. a word used to describe a verb, an adjective, or an adverb

8. a printed sheet with spaces to write information

Number Sense?

English is not the only subject in which it is important to know and understand vocabulary. Words are important in all subjects. These vocabulary words all relate to math. Read the nouns in the box below. Then, on each line, write the word from the box that names the circled number.

---

dividend (*n.*)—the number divided by another number

divisor (*n.*)—the number that divides another number

product (*n.*)—the number resulting from multiplying two or more
          numbers

quotient (*n.*)—the number resulting from dividing one number by
          another

sum (*n.*)—the number resulting from adding numbers together

---

1. $3\overline{)\textcircled{6}}$ with quotient 2   _____

2. $\begin{array}{r} 5 \\ +\ 7 \\ \hline \textcircled{12} \end{array}$ _____

3. $3\overline{)15}$ with quotient $\textcircled{5}$ _____

4. $\begin{array}{r} 4 \\ \times\ 4 \\ \hline \textcircled{16} \end{array}$ _____

5. $\textcircled{9}\overline{)18}$ with quotient 2   _____

Math Words

More Math

Here are some more math vocabulary words. Read the nouns in the box below. Then label each item with the correct word from the box.

> altogether (*n.*)—on the whole, used as a keyword in addition problems
> difference (*n.*)—remainder or what is left after subtracting one number from another
> height (*n.*)—the distance from the bottom to the top of something standing upright
> total (*n.*)—the entire amount; the result of addition
> width (*n.*)—the shortest or shorter side of an object

1.

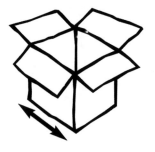

_____

2.

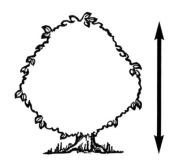

_____

3.

$$\begin{array}{r} 2 \\ +\ 2 \\ \hline ④ \end{array}$$

_____

4.

$$\begin{array}{r} 10 \\ -\ 6 \\ \hline ④ \end{array}$$

_____

5. If Carlos had three apples and two oranges, how many pieces of fruit did he have _____?

Sentenced to Math

Fill in each line with the word from the box that best completes the sentence.

altogether	dividend	height	quotient	total
difference	divisor	product	sum	width

1. We need to know the _____ of the bookcase to be sure it won't hit the ceiling.

2. A number divided by another number is a _____

3. If you multiply these numbers together, you will find the _____.

4. Three is the _____ between seven and four.

5. The three keywords that have to do with addition are _____, _____, and _____.

6. I have already measured the length and height of the bureau, but I still need the _____.

7. A number that divides into another number is the _____.

8. Two is the _____ if you divide eight by four.

Does It Add Up?

Write a sentence using each word pair.

1. find/sum _____

   _____

2. test/product _____

   _____

3. answer/quotient _____

   _____

4. number/divisor _____

   _____

5. whole/dividend _____

   _____

6. problem/altogether _____

   _____

7. left/difference _____

   _____

8. count/total _____

   _____

9. wonder/height _____

   _____

10. narrow/width _____

   _____

Daily Skill-Builders Vocabulary 4–5
walch.com © 2004 Walch Publishing

Math Words

Taking Measurements

We often use **adjectives** to describe how large or how small something is. To give specific measurements, we use words such as these. Read the nouns in the box below. Then fill in each line with the word from the box that best completes the sentence.

distance (n.)—how far two points or places are from each other
interval (n.)—a space of time between events or states of mind
length (n.)—the distance from one end to the other of the longer or
      longest side of an object
temperature (n.)—a measurement in degrees of heat or cold, as
      indicated by a thermometer
volume (n.)—space included within limits as measured in cubic units

1. Please take my _____, because I feel hot.

2. To buy the right size carpet, we must measure the _____ from the door to the window and from the near wall to the far one.

3. I wonder if my arms are the same _____.

4. The bell rings at a regular _____ to signal the end of class.

5. Today we learned how to find the _____ of a drinking glass.

Great Lengths

There are many units of measurement in the world. One system of measurement is the English system, which is the system commonly used in the United States. In many other countries, and in science, the metric system is used.

These words are units used to measure length and distance. Read the nouns in the box below. Then list two things that you could measure using each unit of measurement.

---

foot (*n*.)—an English unit of measurement equal to 12 inches

inch (*n*.)—a small English unit of measurement

meter (*n*.)—the main unit of measurement in the metric system equal to about 39.37 English inches

mile (*n*.)—an English unit of measurement equal to 1760 yards or 5280 feet

yard (*n*.)—an English unit of measurement equal to 3 feet or 36 inches

---

1. inch _____ _____

2. foot _____ _____

3. yard _____ _____

4. mile _____ _____

5. meter _____ _____

Long-Distance Relationships

Think about each pair of words. Explain the relationship between the words in each pair.

1. yard/meter _____

_____

2. inch/foot _____

_____

3. mile/distance _____

_____

4. length/interval _____

_____

5. temperature/volume _____

_____

More Than a Measurement?

Some words have more than one meaning, or **multiple meanings.** For example, a *foot* is a unit of measurement that equals 12 inches. It is also the part of the body at the end of the leg.

Write a meaning for each vocabulary word that is different from the one you have learned in this lesson. Use a dictionary for help.

1. length _____

_____

2. volume _____

_____

3. distance _____

_____

4. inch _____

_____

5. yard _____

_____

6. meter _____

_____

Daily Skill-Builders Vocabulary 4–5
walch.com © 2004 Walch Publishing

Measurement Words

Fill It Up!

Here are more measurement words. You may use these in the kitchen, in the supermarket, and in other everyday places. Read the nouns in the box below. Then list the units that might be used to measure each item. More than one word may be correct.

---

cup (*n.*)—an English measurement; the amount generally held by a cup; 8 ounces or $\frac{1}{2}$ pint

pint (*n.*)—an English unit of measurement equal to two cupfuls or $\frac{1}{2}$ quart or 16 ounces

quart (*n.*)—an English unit of measurement that equals 4 cups or two pints or $\frac{1}{4}$ gallon

gallon (*n.*)—an English unit of measurement for liquid that equals 4 quarts

liter (*n.*)—a metric unit of measurement for liquids; 1 liter = 1.057 quarts

---

1. milk_____

2. sugar for a recipe_____

3. ice cream_____

4. gasoline_____

5. coffee in the morning_____

6. water in a swimming pool _____

English and Metric Measurement

Weighty Words

These units are used to measure weight. Read the nouns in the box below. Then list two things you might measure using each unit.

> gram (*n.*)—a very small measure of metric weight equal to $\frac{1}{28}$ of an ounce
>
> ounce (*n.*)—an English unit of measurement equal to about 28 grams or $\frac{1}{16}$ a liquid pint
>
> pound (*n.*)—an English unit of measurement equal to 16 ounces
>
> ton (*n.*)—an English unit of weight equal to 2,000 pounds
>
> weight (*n.*)—a measurement of how heavy an object or amount of something is

1. ounce _____   _____

2. pound _____   _____

3. ton _____   _____

4. gram _____   _____

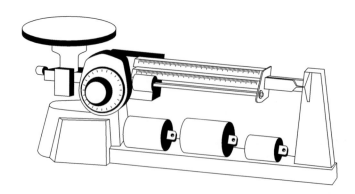

English and Metric Measurement

How Much Is Enough?

Read each definition. In the spaces, write the letters of the correct vocabulary word from the box.

cup	gram	ounce	pound	ton
gallon	liter	pint	quart	weight

1. a metric unit just larger than a quart   _ _ _ _ _

2. how heavy an object or amount is   _ _ _ _ _ _

3. an English unit equal to 8 ounces or $\frac{1}{2}$ pint   _ _ _

4. a very small metric unit equal to $\frac{1}{28}$ ounce   _ _ _ _

5. an English unit equal to 4 cups or 2 pints   _ _ _ _ _

6. an English unit equal to 16 ounces   _ _ _ _ _

7. an English unit equal to 4 quarts   _ _ _ _ _ _

8. an English unit equal to 2,000 pounds   _ _ _

9. an English unit equal to 2 cupfuls or $\frac{1}{2}$ quart   _ _ _ _

10. an English unit equal to about 28 grams   _ _ _ _ _

English and Metric Measurement

What a Mess!

Unscramble each vocabulary word, and write it on the line. Then draw a line from each unscrambled word to its definition.

1. olagln _____

2. rqatu _____

3. pcu _____

4. agmr _____

5. cnoue _____

6. nodup _____

7. otn _____

8. trile _____

9. nipt _____

10. hewtig _____

a. an English unit equal to 16 ounces

b. an English unit equal to 2,000 pounds

c. how heavy an object or amount is

d. an English unit equal to 4 quarts

e. an English unit equal to 2 cups or $\frac{1}{2}$ quart

f. a metric unit just larger than a quart

g. a metric unit equal to $\frac{1}{28}$ of an ounce

h. an English unit equal to 28 grams

i. an English unit equal to 8 ounces or $\frac{1}{2}$ pint

j. an English unit equal to 4 cups or 2 pints

English and Metric Measurement

Unit 1 Review

A. Follow the directions for each item.

1. Define the word *simile*. _____

_____

2. Write two similes of your own. _____

_____

_____

B. Circle the letter of the word that does not belong. On the line, write why that word does not belong.

1. **a.** define   **b.** atlas   **c.** dictionary   **d.** pronoun

_____

2. **a.** astronomy   **b.** biology   **c.** geology   **d.** science

_____

3. **a.** principal   **b.** mathematics **c.** temperature   **d.** inch

_____

4. **a.** liter   **b.** gram   **c.** meter   **d.** yard

_____

5. **a.** application   **b.** form   **c.** composition   **d.** comma

_____

Unit 1 Review, cont.

C. Write a sentence using each vocabulary word.

1. janitor _____

2. product _____

3. chemistry _____

4. pound _____

5. outline_____

6. auditorium _____

7. volume _____

8. adverb_____

9. library _____

10. history_____

D. In your own words, write the definition of each word below.

1. research_____

2. volunteer_____

3. interval _____

4. quotient _____

5. dividend _____

Everyday People

Here are some nouns that we use to name people. Read the nouns in the box below. Then answer each item. If you need additional space, use another sheet of paper.

adult (*n*.)—a fully developed and mature person
pupil (*n*.)—a student
partner (*n*.)—a person who does or shares something with someone else
neighbor (*n*.)—a person living near or next to another
human (*n*.)—a person

1. Name an adult who is important to you. Then tell why that person is important. _____

_____

2. Write a sentence using the word *pupil*. _____

_____

3. List three things for which you would need a partner. _____

_____

4. What kinds of things does someone do for a neighbor? _____

_____

5. What does it mean to be a human? _____

_____

Family Members

Here are some nouns that name family members. Read the nouns in the box below. Then write a sentence using each word pair.

> parent (*n.*)—a father or mother of a child
> aunt (*n.*)—the sister of a parent or the wife of an uncle
> uncle (*n.*)—the brother of a parent or the husband of an aunt
> grandmother (*n.*)—the mother of one's mother or father
> grandfather (*n.*)—the father of one's mother or father

1. parent/important _____

_____

2. aunt/holidays _____

_____

3. uncle/teaching _____

_____

4. grandmother/playing _____

_____

5. grandfather/spoil_____

_____

People in Our Lives

People Puzzle

Match each clue with a vocabulary word from the box. Write the vocabulary word in the puzzle.

adult	grandfather	human	parent	pupil
aunt	grandmother	neighbor	partner	uncle

Across

2. a fully developed and mature person
5. the brother of a parent or the husband of an aunt
7. a father or mother
8. the sister of a parent or the wife of an uncle
10. the mother of one's mother or father

Down

1. a student
3. the father of one's mother or father
4. a person who does or shares something with someone else
6. a person living near or next to another
9. a person

Tell Me About It!

Write a descriptive paragraph about something funny that happened to you.
Use at least five words from the box.

adult	partner	human	uncle	grandmother
pupil	neighbor	aunt	parent	grandfather

_____

_____

_____

_____

_____

_____

_____

_____

_____

_____

Verb Movement

These verbs all have to do with body movements. Read the verbs in the box below. Then fill in each line with the word from the box that best completes the sentence.

blink (v.)—to shut and open the eyes quickly
swallow (v.)—to take into the stomach through the mouth and throat
faint (v.)—to lose consciousness briefly
sniff (v.)—to smell by taking short breaths in through the nose
twitch (v.)—to move or pull with a sudden motion; to jerk

1. Just as I was about to fall asleep, my leg began to

   _____.

2. I bent to _____ the flowers, but
   they were plastic!

3. When I walked from the dark auditorium into the bright
   light, I had to _____ many times.

4. Teresa felt as though she would _____ from the
   shock of the accident.

5. A sore throat makes it hard to _____.

Body Words

Body Language

The human body has ways of telling us what we need. These nouns all represent methods that the body uses to tell us something is wrong. Read the nouns in the box below. Then fill in each line with the word from the box that best completes the sentence.

> hunger (*n.*)—a desire or need for food
> thirst (*n.*)—a feeling of dryness in the mouth and throat that indicates a need for liquid to drink
> sweat (*n.*)—the moisture coming from or collecting in drops on the skin
> fever (*n.*)—the rise of the body temperature above normal
> swelling (*n.*)—the expanding of a body part

1. The _____ of her arm told Rena that her wrist was sprained.

2. _____ dripped from the players as they ran in the hot sun.

3. _____ drove the lost boy to drink from a puddle.

4. Noah's _____ was rising, so he took a cool bath.

5. After a day without food, the _____ made Nancy's stomach ache.

Crossed Signals

Match each clue with a vocabulary word from the box. Write the vocabulary word in the puzzle.

blink	fever	sniff	sweat	thirst
faint	hunger	swallow	swelling	twitch

Across

3. the moisture coming from or collecting in drops on the skin
4. to shut and open the eyes quickly
5. to jerk
7. to smell by taking short breaths in through the nose
8. the expanding of a body part
9. the rise of the body temperature above normal

Down

1. to take into the stomach through the mouth and throat
2. to lose consciousness briefly
5. a feeling of dryness in the mouth and throat that indicates a need to drink
6. a desire or need for food

Body Words

So Many Symptoms!

Read each definition. On the line, write the correct word from the box.

blink	faint	twitch	thirst	fever
swallow	sniff	hunger	sweat	swelling

1. the moisture coming from or collecting in drops on the surface of the skin _____

2. to lose consciousness briefly _____

3. to move or pull with a sudden motion; to jerk _____

4. a desire or need for food _____

5. the expanding of a body part _____

6. to take into the stomach through the mouth and throat _____

7. the rise of the body temperature above normal _____

8. to smell by taking short breaths in through the nose _____

9. to shut and open the eyes quickly _____

10. a feeling of dryness in the mouth and throat that indicates a need for liquid to drink _____

Body Words

Where Will They Take You?

There are many names for parts of the human body. These five nouns are simply major parts of the leg. Read the nouns in the box below. Then fill in each line with the word from the box that best completes the sentence.

> tendon (*n.*)—a tough band of tissue that joins muscle with
>   another body part, such as a bone
> shin (*n.*)—the front part of the leg below the knee
> calf (*n.*)—the muscular back part of the leg below the knee
> kneecap (*n.*)—a thick, flat, moveable bone forming the front
>   part of the knee
> ankle (*n.*)—the joint between the foot and the leg

1. Matt was afraid he might get a cramp in his _____ so he did not go swimming.

2. Emily twisted her _____ and had to drop out of the race.

3. When Grammy fell, she cracked her _____ and could not bend her leg.

4. The wild soccer ball slammed my _____ and left a bruise below my knee.

5. Lexie tore her Achilles' _____, which joins the heel and the leg muscle.

Parts of the Body

Anatomy Lesson

Here are some more nouns that name other parts of the body. Read the nouns in the box below. Then fill in each line with the word from the box that best completes the sentence.

> organ (*n.*)—a part of the body that is specialized to do a particular task
> chest (*n.*)—the part of the body enclosed by the ribs and breastbone
> skull (*n.*)—the case of bone that forms the skeleton of the head and
>   face and encloses the brain
> forehead (*n.*)—the part of the face above the eyes
> limb (*n.*)—an arm or a leg

1. Pain in the _____ can be a sign of a heart attack.

2. If a major _____ fails, an operation may be needed.

3. The _____ helps protect the brain, but a helmet is still needed for safety.

4. I'm getting a line across my _____ from frowning so much.

5. A soldier lost a(n) _____ when a mine exploded near him.

Parts of the Body

More Anatomy

Label each body part with a word from the box.

tendon	calf	ankle	chest	limb
shin	kneecap	organ	skull	forehead

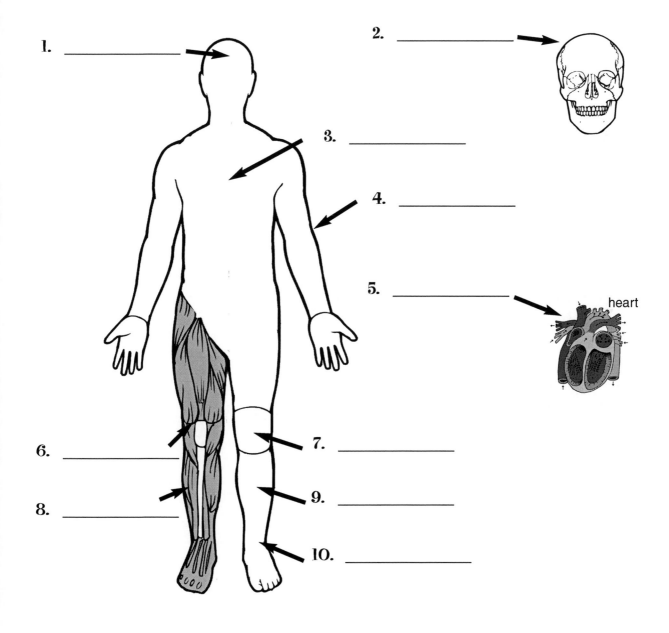

1. _____

2. _____

3. _____

4. _____

5. _____

6. _____

7. _____

8. _____

9. _____

10. _____

heart

Parts of the Body

Parts of a Whole

Read each definition. In the spaces, write the letters of the correct vocabulary word from the box.

tendon	calf	ankle	chest	limb
shin	kneecap	organ	skull	forehead

1. the joint between the foot and the leg   _ _ _ _ _

2. an arm or a leg   _ _ _ _

3. a part of the body that is specialized to do a particular task   _ _ _ _ _

4. a tough band that joins muscle with another body part, such as bone   _ _ _ _ _ _

5. the case of bone that forms the skeleton of the head and face and encloses the brain   _ _ _ _ _

6. a bone forming the front part of the knee   _ _ _ _ _ _ _

7. the part of the body enclosed by the ribs and breastbone   _ _ _ _ _

8. the muscular back part of the leg   _ _ _ _

9. the part of the face above the eyes   _ _ _ _ _ _ _ _

10. the front part of the leg below the knee   _ _ _ _

Daily Skill-Builders Vocabulary 4–5
walch.com © 2004 Walch Publishing

Clean and Healthy

Cleanliness is an important part in keeping the body healthy. These words are all key elements of good health. Read the words in the box below. Then write a sentence using each word pair.

hygiene (n.)—actions (such as keeping clean) that lead to good health
bathe (v.)—to wash
disinfect (v.)—to destroy germs on
dress (v.)—to apply medicine and a bandage to an injured body part
bandage (n.)—a strip of cloth or latex used to bind wounds

1. bathe/daily _____

   _____

2. disinfect/tweezers _____

   _____

3. dress/cut _____

   _____

4. bandage/wound _____

   _____

5. hygiene/follow _____

   _____

Hygiene Words

Clean Up Your Act!

These words are things we do or use to keep clean. Read the words in the box below. Then fill in each line with the word from the box that best completes the sentence.

> floss (*v.*)—to pass special dental thread through the teeth
> gargle (*v.*)—to swirl liquid around in the mouth and throat
> lather (*n.*)—foam
> deodorant (*n.*)—a product that masks or destroys unpleasant odors
> groom (*v.*)—to make neat and attractive

1. I sometimes _____ with salt water if my throat is sore.

2. This _____ does not work very well through gym class.

3. I _____ twice a day because I have gaps in my teeth that trap food.

4. It takes my brother hours to _____ himself before school.

5. The advertisement promises that the shampoo produces thick _____.

Hygiene Words

Squeaky Clean

Write the definition of each vocabulary word. Then circle each vocabulary word in the word search. Words appear across or down.

1. floss _____
2. gargle _____
3. lather _____
4. deodorant _____
5. groom _____
6. hygiene _____
7. bathe _____
8. disinfect _____
9. dress _____
10. bandage _____

```
H E M O U T H L U L L A N D A
B Y F C L E A N S P I C A N D
S P A N S P O T L E S S F I L
M A C U L A T E B P U R L E P
E R D E O D O R A N T F O C T
A N T I D B A C T E R I S A L
H A N D R W A S H I N G S O A
P I N A E P U M E P B O T T L
E O R I S B A N D A G E N A B
A R O R S P E R H G R O O M A
P H Y G I E N E C S S O M E K
N D G A R G L E L A T H E R F
P E R D F U E M E T D N S C E
C A T N D S L E T A R E A B I
D I S I N F E C T I O N O F T
```

Hygiene Words

Rise and Shine

Write a paragraph about getting ready in the morning. Use at least five words from the box.

| bandage | deodorant | dress | gargle | hygiene |
| bathe | disinfect | floss | groom | lather |

_____

_____

_____

_____

_____

_____

_____

_____

_____

_____

_____

Hygiene Words

Who Are You?

People are made up of more than body parts. These nouns name qualities that are part of who we are. Read the nouns in the box below. Then fill in each line with the word from the box that best completes the sentence.

> character (n.)—the mental and moral qualities that
> make a person different from others
> behavior (n.)—the way someone acts
> nature (n.)—the basic personality of a person
> attitude (n.)—an opinion about a particular situation
> appearance (n.)—how someone looks

1. Cassie's _____ has changed since she gained weight and cut her hair.

2. Keisha's _____ toward her stepdad changed after she got to know him.

3. That wild _____ is no way to act in the classroom!

4. Drew's gentle _____ draws animals to him.

5. The company asked about the man's _____ before they hired him as a security guard.

Character Words

How Others See Us

These words have to do with how people feel about other people. Read the words in the box below. Then fill in each line with the word from the box that best completes the sentence.

> admire (*v.*)—to think very highly of and respect
> dislike (*v.*)—to not like; to not care for something
> disappointed (*adj.*)—having one's desires not met
> proud (*adj.*)—having a feeling of pleasure with oneself or
>   for another
> approve (*v.*)—to think well of; to accept

1. I _____ the way that the salesperson spoke to us. Let's go to another store.

2. Jamie's parents are _____ of her for working hard in school.

3. The children were _____ that the trip was canceled.

4. Mom does not always _____ of my music!

5. I _____ Kenji for his hard work.

Character Words

Working Together

Write a sentence using each word pair.

1. admire/character _____

_____

2. dislike/attitude _____

_____

3. approve/nature _____

_____

4. proud/behavior _____

_____

5. disappointed/appearance _____

_____

Now write a definition for the opposite of the following word.

6. approve _____

_____

Character Words

Progress Report

Imagine you are a fourth-grade teacher. You are writing progress reports for your students. Write a report here for a boy or a girl in your class. Use five words from the box.

| appearance | behavior | nature | dislike | proud |
| attitude | character | admire | disappointed | approve |

Dear Parents,

_____

_____

_____

_____

_____

_____

_____

_____

_____

_____

_____

_____

Sincerely,

_____

Daily Skill-Builders Vocabulary 4–5
walch.com © 2004 Walch Publishing

Character Words

Something to Read

There are many different things to read. The following nouns are some of those things. Read the nouns in the box below. Then fill in each line with the word from the box that best completes the sentence.

> newspaper (*n.*)—a paper printed and sold, usually daily or weekly, that includes reports of recent events, articles of opinion, and other types of writing
>
> magazine (*n.*)—a weekly or monthly publication with pictures and articles
>
> catalog (*n.*)—a list of names, titles, or objects arranged in an order, often published for sale
>
> article (*n.*)—a piece of writing, not fiction or poetry, that forms a part of a larger publication such as a newspaper or magazine
>
> chapter (*n.*)—a main division of a book or story

1. Dad would like to order something from the _____ that he received in the mail.

2. Billy read an interesting _____ in the paper at breakfast.

3. I have to read one more _____ before I go to bed. We're having a quiz in the morning.

4. Michelle loved the _____ about movie stars.

5. The headline in the _____ was about the big game.

Tools of the Trade

These nouns name things some people use for work. Read the nouns in the box below. Then fill in each line with the word from the box that best completes the sentence.

---

network (n.)—a system of computers connected by communication
lines

keyboard (n.)—an arrangement of keys that print letters when pressed

calculator (n.)—a device for doing mathematical functions

tote (n.)—a large carrying bag

agenda (n.)—a list or an outline of things to be done

---

1. Cal looked at the _____ to find out how many topics were to be covered.

2. Lani typed the list of names on the _____.

3. Because the _____ was down, Linda could not get her e-mail.

4. Darren carried all his papers and books in a large _____.

5. Juanita used her _____ to figure out the total number.

Reading and Business Words

Match 'Em

Below are vocabulary words and definitions. Find the definition of each vocabulary word. Write the letter of the correct definition on the line.

1. _____ newspaper

2. _____ magazine

3. _____ catalog

4. _____ article

5. _____ chapter

6. _____ network

7. _____ keyboard

8. _____ calculator

9. _____ tote

10. _____ agenda

a. a piece of writing that forms part of a larger publication, such as a newspaper or a magazine

b. a list or an outline of things to be done

c. a weekly or monthly publication issued with pictures and articles

d. a system of computers connected by communication lines

e. written material printed and sold every day or week with reports of recent events, opinions, and other writing

f. an arrangement of keys that print letters when pressed

g. a main division of a book or story

h. a list of names, titles, or objects arranged in an order, often published for sale

i. a device for doing mathematical functions

j. a large carrying bag

Reading and Business Words

Working Words

Write the definition of each vocabulary word. Then circle each vocabulary word in the word search. Words appear across, down, or diagonally.

1. newspaper _____

2. network _____

3. magazine _____

4. keyboard _____

5. catalog _____

6. agenda _____

7. article _____

8. calculator _____

9. chapter _____

10. tote _____

```
N E W S P A P E R T O T E B A
A V A N T D E P A R T I C R I
L F C A U T A Q U E T U A F A
S S A E M L A G V A I S L S E
L L T E D A C C E O R D C O U
N O A N S I G T U N P R U E F
A E L R E S O A N P D E L U T
R R O E S T E R Z I C A A I T
T C G O U T E L A I N U T I T
I T H I S I S N O T N A O H A
C T H A I S I S A P I E R C T
L U R E P O F A H A T C E C I
E N E S T T P A S U N C H A P
E A U C E S E N E T W O R K T
U K E Y B O A R D N I M A G E
```

Daily Skill-Builders Vocabulary 4–5
walch.com © 2004 Walch Publishing

Reading and Business Words

Light Reading

We read every day—not just in school. These vocabulary words are items people read. Read the nouns in the box below. Then explain when or why you would read each item.

receipt (*n.*)—a printed document noting money received
manual (*n.*)—a book that explains or tells how to use something
cookbook (*n.*)—a book of recipes and directions
invitation (*n.*)—a written note asking someone to come to an
        occasion
correspondence (*n.*)—letters

1. receipt _____

_____

2. manual _____

_____

3. cookbook _____

_____

4. invitation _____

_____

5. correspondence _____

_____

Hard Work = Benefits

Students work hard in school. People work hard at jobs. These nouns are some results of hard work. Read the nouns in the box below. Then write a sentence using each word pair.

acceptance (*n.*)—the state of being found worthy and received
           willingly
position (*n.*)—a job
options (*n.*)—possibilities; choices
compliment (*n.*)—expression of praise, respect, or admiration
reward (*n.*)—something given or offered in return for special service

1. peers/acceptance _____

_____

2. graduate/position _____

_____

3. effort/options _____

_____

4. respect/compliments _____

_____

5. work/reward _____

_____

Reasons for Learning

Look and Learn

Unscramble each vocabulary word, and write it on the short line. Then write the definition of the word on the long line.

1. nlomecpimt _____

_____

2. naulma _____

_____

3. cecantapec _____

_____

4. eireptc _____

_____

5. niatovtini _____

_____

6. opiistno _____

_____

7. werdar _____

_____

8. porrocnsedcene _____

_____

9. koboocko _____

_____

10. snopoit _____

_____

Reasons for Learning

It's All About You!

Write a sentence about your life using each word.

1. receipt _____

_____

2. manual _____

_____

3. cookbook _____

_____

4. invitation _____

_____

5. correspondence _____

_____

6. acceptance _____

_____

7. position _____

_____

8. options _____

_____

9. compliment _____

_____

10. reward _____

_____

Daily Skill-Builders Vocabulary 4–5
walch.com © 2004 Walch Publishing

Reasons for Learning

Unit 2 Review

A. Circle the letter of the word that does not belong. On the line, tell why that word does not belong.

1. **a.** admire   **b.** acceptance   **c.** disappointed   **d.** compliment

   _____

2. **a.** calf   **b.** shin   **c.** forehead   **d.** kneecap

   _____

3. **a.** swallow   **b.** twitch   **c.** blink   **d.** tendon

   _____

4. **a.** hygiene   **b.** bathe   **c.** organ   **d.** disinfect

   _____

5. **a.** character   **b.** nature   **c.** attitude   **d.** appearance

   _____

B. Find the definition for each vocabulary word. Write the letter of the correct definition on the line.

1. _____ article

2. _____ chapter

3. _____ agenda

4. _____ invitation

5. _____ manual

a. a list or an outline of things to be done

b. a note asking someone to come to an occasion

c. a main division of a book or story

d. a piece of writing, not fiction or poetry, that forms part of a larger publication

e. a book that explains or tells how to use something

Unit 2 Review, cont.

C. Write the definition of each word.

1. receipt _____

2. network _____

3. correspondence _____

4. reward _____

5. options _____

D. Write a sentence for each word.

1. invitation _____

2. proud _____

3. behavior _____

4. fever _____

5. dislike _____

6. limb _____

7. nature _____

8. partner _____

9. dress _____

10. position _____

Daily Skill-Builders Vocabulary 4–5
walch.com © 2004 Walch Publishing

Unit 2 Review

Sense of Taste

These words are all **adjectives**, or describing words. They describe how things taste. Read the adjectives in the box below. Then list two foods that could be described by each adjective.

salty (*adj.*)—tasting like or containing salt, a white substance
used to season and preserve foods
sweet (*adj.*)—tasting like sugar
bitter (*adj.*)—sharp, biting, and unpleasant to the taste
sour (*adj.*)—having an acid or a spoiled taste
delicious (*adj.*)—giving great pleasure, especially to taste or smell

1. salty _____ _____

2. sweet _____ _____

3. bitter _____ _____

4. sour _____ _____

5. delicious _____ _____

Now use two of the words above in sentences of your own.

_____

_____

_____

_____

Comparing Tastes

Let's Compare

Explaining something is easier when you can compare it to something else. These vocabulary words help you compare things. Read the words in the box below. Then write a sentence for each word.

> similar (*adj.*)—having qualities in common
> unlike (*adj.*)—different; unequal; not the same
> differences (*n.*)—what makes two or more things not the same
> vary (*v.*)—to make or be of different kinds
> identical (*adj.*)—being exactly alike, equal, or the same

1. similar _____

   _____

2. unlike _____

   _____

3. differences _____

   _____

4. vary _____

   _____

5. identical _____

   _____

Comparing Tastes

Similar Tastes

Write the definition of each vocabulary word. Then circle each vocabulary word in the word search. Words appear across, down, or diagonally.

1. salty _____

2. similar _____

3. sweet _____

4. unlike_____

5. bitter _____

6. differences _____

7. sour _____

8. vary _____

9. delicious_____

10. identical_____

```
V A R S U F S I M T T E R D V
Y C T A T F U L V E F F I I T
S K D L S C I S A L D E D F C
A U N T W F F E R E N C E F Y
L U N Y E K L S V T T C N E K
O F F P E T I D O O R S T R U
O F W I T I K M I U V R I E N
B I T T E R V A R R R K C N D
D I C I O S A L D K A T A C S
S W A L F F R T W T Y A L E A
O V S I M I L A R S H A R S D
S A L S W S C A R L T F L U V
T R F A F O W L U N L I K E E
E Y E L I T E B O O K F A C R
O L E D R E D E L I C I O U S
```

Comparing Tastes

Taste and Compare

Read each definition. In the spaces, write the correct vocabulary word from the box.

salty	bitter	delicious	unlike	vary
sweet	sour	similar	differences	identical

1. to make or be of different kinds   _ _ _ _

2. having qualities in common   _ _ _ _ _ _ _

3. tasting like a white substance that seasons or preserves food   _ _ _ _ _ _

4. giving great pleasure, especially to taste or smell   _ _ _ _ _ _ _ _ _

5. different; unequal; not the same   _ _ _ _ _ _

6. having an acid or spoiled taste   _ _ _ _

7. being exactly alike or the same   _ _ _ _ _ _ _ _ _

8. sharp, biting, unpleasant to taste   _ _ _ _ _ _

9. what makes two or more things not the same   _ _ _ _ _ _ _ _ _ _ _

10. something that tastes like sugar   _ _ _ _ _

Move It!

These words are about moving. Read the words in the box below. Then fill in each line with the word from the box that best completes the sentence.

> stationary (*adj.*)—not changing or moving
> crawled (*v*)—moved slowly with the body on hands and knees
> tumble (*v.*)—to fall suddenly and helplessly, rolling and turning
> sliding (*v.*)—moving; gliding; passing smoothly over a surface
> bounce (*v.*)—to spring back or up after hitting a surface

1. When no one is watching, I love to _____ on my bed.

2. This exercise bike is _____. It never actually leaves the room!

3. The baby _____ across the room to us. She will learn to walk soon.

4. Brad was _____ across the pond—without skates!

5. If my foot slips, I will _____ down the hill.

Movement Words

Moving Pictures

Here are more verbs about moving. Read the verbs in the box below. Then fill in each line with the word from the box that best completes the sentence.

> flipped (v.)—moved or turned by tossing end over end
> jog (v.)—to run at a slow, easy pace
> sprint (v.)—to run at top speed, usually for a short distance
> raced (v.)—went, moved, or drove at top speed
> gallop (v.)—to go or run in a fast, springing manner, like a horse

1. Tran _____ a coin to choose which movie to see.

2. I _____ around the track to warm up for a game.

3. The car _____ across the finish line.

4. I save my energy at the start, and then I _____ at the end of a race.

5. The horse will _____ too quickly if you frighten him.

A **synonym** is a word that has almost the same meaning as another word. *Chilly* and *cool* are synonyms.

Write a synonym for each vocabulary word below.

6. flipped   _____

7. raced   _____

8. stationary   _____

9. tumble   _____

10. sliding   _____

Movement Words

Moving Word Pairs

Read each word pair. Explain how the two words in each pair are related.

1. stationary/crawled _____

   _____

2. tumble/bounce _____

   _____

3. sprint/raced _____

   _____

   _____

4. jog/gallop _____

   _____

5. flipped/sliding _____

   _____

Movement Words

Amazing Race

Write a letter to a friend about a race you saw. Use at least five words from the box.

stationary	tumble	bounce	jog	sprint
crawled	sliding	flipped	gallop	raced

Dear _____,

_____

_____

_____

_____

_____

_____

_____

_____

_____

_____

_____

Yours Truly,

_____

Movement Words

Not-so-Straight

These adjectives describe things that are not straight. Read the adjectives in the box below. Then write a sentence using each word pair.

> curly (*adj.*)—having coils or twists that form ringlets
> crooked (*adj.*)—not straight
> curved (*adj.*)—bending or turning without angles
> spiral (*adj.*)—circling around a center and gradually
> getting closer to or farther away from it
> circular (*adj.*)—having the form of a circle

1. hair/curly _____

_____

2. shelf/crooked _____

_____

3. driveway/curved _____

_____

4. decorations/spiral _____

_____

5. building/circular _____

_____

How Does It Look?

These words are all about how something appears. Read the words in the box below. Then list two things that fit each word.

> colorful (*adj.*)—having bright colors
> foggy (*adj.*)—filled with clouds of moisture that stay
> close to the ground
> blur (*n.*)—something that cannot be seen clearly
> excellent (*adj.*)—very good; the best quality
> spotless (*adj.*)—perfectly clean or pure; free from markings

1. colorful _____ _____

2. foggy _____ _____

3. blur _____ _____

4. excellent _____ _____

5. spotless _____ _____

Now use two words from above in sentences of your own.

_____

_____

_____

_____

Describing Words

Choose a Letter!

Below are vocabulary words and definitions. Find the definition of each vocabulary word. Write the letter of the correct definition on the line.

1. _____ curly

2. _____ circular

3. _____ crooked

4. _____ curved

5. _____ spiral

6. _____ colorful

7. _____ foggy

8. _____ blur

9. _____ excellent

10. _____ spotless

a. having bright colors

b. bending or turning without angles

c. perfectly clean or pure; free from markings

d. having coils or twists that form ringlets

e. filled with clouds of moisture that stay close to the ground

f. not straight

g. something that cannot be seen clearly

h. having the form of a circle

i. circling around a center and slowly getting closer to or farther away from it

j. very good; the best quality

Crossroads

Match each clue with a vocabulary word from the box. Write the vocabulary word in the puzzle.

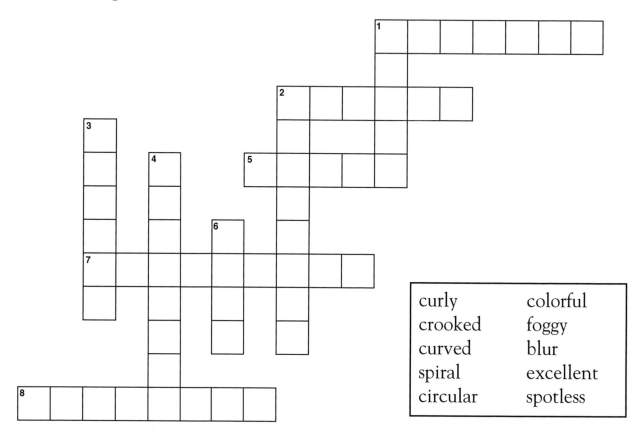

curly	colorful
crooked	foggy
curved	blur
spiral	excellent
circular	spotless

Across

1. not straight
2. circling around a center and getting closer to or farther from it
5. filled with clouds of moisture that stay close to the ground
7. very good
8. having bright colors

Down

1. having coils that form ringlets
2. perfectly clean or pure
3. bending or turning without angles
4. having the form of a circle
6. something not seen clearly

Describing Words

How Does It Feel?

Human beings have five senses. One of these is the sense of touch. These adjectives describe how things feel to the touch. Read the adjectives in the box below. Then fill in each line with the word from the box that best completes the sentence.

firm (*adj.*)—having a solid, compact texture
softest (*adj.*)—the least hard or solid
coarse (*adj.*)—being harsh or rough
tender (*adj.*)—delicate; not tough
roughest (*adj.*)—most rugged in nature or look

1. This pillow is the _____ I have ever slept on.

2. The ground here is _____. It will be tough to dig.

3. The _____ sandpaper could not rub the paint off.

4. The _____ sand hurt my bare feet.

5. The _____ skin around the eyes is easily bruised.

An **antonym** is a word that means almost the opposite of another word. *Happy* and *sad* are antonyms.

Write an antonym for each vocabulary word below.

6. tender   _____

7. coarse   _____

8. firm   _____

9. softest   _____

10. roughest _____

Ouch and Yuck!

Here are more adjectives about how things feel to the touch. Read the adjectives in the box below. Then write the word from the box that best fits each description.

> jagged (*adj.*)—having a sharp or an uneven edge or surface
> bumpy (*adj.*)—unevenness; having small, rounded lumps
> sticky (*adj.*)—coated with an adhesive substance
> squishy (*adj.*)—soft and pulpy
> slippery (*adj.*)—having a surface smooth or wet enough
>   to make something slide

1. a raised rash   _____

2. a wet pool slide   _____

3. a dried juice spill   _____

4. gravel on a path   _____

5. mud between your toes   _____

Now use two words from the box above in sentences of your own.

_____

_____

_____

_____

Touchy Adjectives

List two things that you would describe with each word.

1. firm   _____   _____

2. softest   _____   _____

3. coarse   _____   _____

4. tender   _____   _____

5. roughest   _____   _____

6. jagged   _____   _____

7. bumpy   _____   _____

8. sticky   _____   _____

9. squishy   _____   _____

10. slippery   _____   _____

Our Senses

75

Pair 'Em Up!

Write a sentence using each word pair.

1. couch/firm _____

   _____

2. shirt/softest _____

   _____

3. surface/coarse _____

   _____

4. bruise/tender _____

   _____

5. tissue/roughest _____

   _____

6. broken/jagged _____

   _____

7. road/bumpy _____

   _____

8. table/sticky _____

   _____

9. shoes/squishy _____

   _____

10. stairs/slippery _____

    _____

To What Degree?

The following adjectives describe different levels within a range. Read the adjectives in the box below. Then write a sentence using each word pair.

> mild (*adj.*)—gentle; not strong or harsh
> moderate (*adj.*)—neither very good nor very bad
> severe (*adj.*)—very strict or harsh
> minor (*adj.*)—small in size, value, or importance
> major (*adj.*)—great in number, quantity, or importance

1. mild/taste _____

_____

2. moderate/ability _____

_____

3. severe/weather _____

_____

4. minor/issue _____

_____

5. major/problem _____

_____

Speedy Words

These words are all about speed. Read the words in the box below. Then write a sentence using each word.

> accelerate (*v.*)—to increase speed; to cause to move faster
> slowest (*adj.*)—moving at a speed less than usual or the rest
> quickest (*adj.*)—fastest; speediest
> swift (*adj.*)—moving or able to move with great speed
> rapid (*adj.*)—very fast

1. accelerate _____

   _____

2. slowest_____

   _____

3. quickest_____

   _____

4. swift_____

   _____

5. rapid _____

   _____

Degree Words

A Little Shuffle

Unscramble each vocabulary word and write it on the short line. Then write the definition of the word on the long line.

1. pradi _____

_____

2. ereevs _____

_____

3. dmli _____

_____

4. twoless _____

_____

5. ojram _____

_____

6. fstiw _____

_____

7. raelceetca _____

_____

8. cteukisq _____

_____

9. niorm _____

_____

10. deotrema _____

_____

Degree Words

A Big Problem

Imagine that there is some sort of problem in your school or community. Write a letter to the governor of your state explaining what is happening and how bad the problem is. Use at least five words from the box.

mild	severe	major	slowest	swift
moderate	minor	accelerate	quickest	rapid

Dear Governor,

_____

_____

_____

_____

_____

_____

_____

_____

_____

_____

Sincerely,

_____

Daily Skill-Builders Vocabulary 4–5
walch.com © 2004 Walch Publishing

Degree Words

When?

These words are time words. They help to explain when events occur. Read the words in the box below. Then fill in each line with the word from the box that best completes the sentence.

> sooner (*adj.* or *adv.*)—occurring before something was expected
> recent (*adj.*)—having lately happened or occurred
> afterward (*adv.*)—at a later time
> previous (*adj.*)—going before in time or order
> earlier (*adj.* or *adv.*)—near the beginning or before the usual time

1. This cut on my arm is so _____ that it is just starting to heal.

2. I did not want to bother my friend during dinner, so I waited until _____ to call him back.

3. Aisha did her homework _____ so that she would not have to stay up late.

4. His _____ books in the series were more interesting.

5. John would have been here _____, but his bike has a flat tire.

Time Words

How Often?

These words all tell how often something happens without giving dates or times. Read the words in the box below. Then use each word in a sentence telling how often you do something.

> usually (*adj.*)—happens most of the time; normally
> occasional (*adj.*)—happening now and then
> frequent (*adj.*)—happening often
> rarely (*adv.*)—not often at all; almost never
> seldom (*adv.*)—not often

1. usually _____

_____

2. occasional _____

_____

3. frequent _____

_____

4. rarely _____

_____

5. seldom _____

_____

Time Words

A Puzzling Time

Match each clue with a vocabulary word from the box. Write the vocabulary word in the puzzle.

sooner	afterward	earlier	occasional	rarely
recent	previous	usually	frequent	seldom

Across
4. happening often
5. not often
6. not often at all; almost never
7. happening in the beginning or before the usual time
10. happening now and then

Down
1. happens most of the time; normally
2. going before in time or order
3. at a later time
8. having lately happened or occurred
9. occurring before something was expected

Time Words

83

Time Difference

Explain the relationship between the words in each pair.

1. sooner/previous _____

_____

_____

2. earlier/afterward _____

_____

_____

3. recent/frequent _____

_____

_____

4. occasional/rarely _____

_____

_____

5. seldom/usually _____

_____

_____

Daily Skill·Builders Vocabulary 4–5
walch.com © 2004 Walch Publishing

Time Words

How Did It Happen?

There are many factors to consider when describing events. These words all have to do with how something occurred in time or detail. Read the words in the box below. Then fill in each line with the word from the box that best completes the sentence.

gradual (*adj.*)—moving or happening slowly in steps
dramatic (*adj.*)—to an extreme degree; emotionally excessive
somewhat (*adv.*)—to some extent; rather
barely (*adv.*)—hardly; scarcely
uneven (*adj.*)—not even or smooth; varying in quality

1. The movie was _____. It was thrilling at the beginning but boring at the end.

2. Studying can make a _____ difference in grades.

3. The shift from day to night was _____. I did not notice it was dark until I needed to turn on the light.

4. The details of the accident are _____ blurred. I do not remember much.

5. He _____ touched his meal, so I knew he was sick.

Adjectives and Verbs

Changes

These verbs are about changing things. Read the verbs in the box below. Then write a sentence for each word pair.

adjust (*v.*)—to arrange or change in order to make something work correctly

modify (*v.*)—to make changes in something

increase (*v.*)—to make or become greater

decrease (*v.*)—to make or become less

maintain (*v.*)—to keep the same; to keep in a desired state

1. adjust/volume _____

_____

2. modify/fit _____

_____

3. increase/games _____

_____

4. decrease/homework _____

_____

5. maintain/health _____

_____

 Daily Skill-Builders Vocabulary 4–5
walch.com © 2004 Walch Publishing   **Adjectives and Verbs**

Sound Check

Imagine that you are at a concert. Something goes wrong with the speakers. For each word, write a sentence about the problem.

1. gradual _____

_____

2. dramatic _____

_____

3. somewhat _____

_____

4. barely _____

_____

5. uneven _____

_____

6. adjust _____

_____

7. modify _____

_____

8. increase _____

_____

9. decrease _____

_____

10. maintain _____

_____

Adjectives and Verbs

Pairing Up!

Below are vocabulary words and definitions. Find the definition of each vocabulary word. Write the letter of the correct definition on the line.

1. _____ gradual

2. _____ dramatic

3. _____ somewhat

4. _____ barely

5. _____ uneven

6. _____ adjust

7. _____ modify

8. _____ increase

9. _____ decrease

10. _____ maintain

a. hardly; scarcely

b. to make changes in

c. moving or happening slowly in steps or degrees

d. to keep the same; to keep in a desired state

e. to an extreme degree; emotionally excessive

f. to make or become less

g. to some extent; rather

h. not even or smooth; varying in quality

i. to arrange or change in order to make something work correctly

j. to make or become greater

Adjectives and Verbs

Unit 3 Review

A. Answer each question.

1. What is a *synonym*? _____

   _____

2. What is an *antonym*? _____

   _____

B. Circle the letter of the word that does not belong. On the line, tell why that word does not belong.

1. **a.** sooner   **b.** earlier   **c.** afterward   **d.** previous

    _____

2. **a.** identical   **b.** vary   **c.** differences   **d.** unlike

    _____

3. **a.** tender   **b.** coarse   **c.** jagged   **d.** bumpy

    _____

4. **a.** flipped   **b.** stationary   **c.** tumble   **d.** crawled

    _____

5. **a.** roughest   **b.** softest   **c.** slippery   **d.** quickest

    _____

Unit 3 Review, cont.

C. Write one synonym and one antonym for each word.

	Synonym	Antonym
1. excellent	_____	_____
2. swift	_____	_____
3. minor	_____	_____
4. modify	_____	_____
5. increase	_____	_____

D. Write a sentence using each word.

1. accelerate _____

_____

2. seldom_____

_____

3. severe _____

_____

4. maintain _____

_____

5. gradual _____

_____

Good Times

These words are about having fun! Read the words in the box below. Then write a sentence using each word pair.

> excited (*adj.*)—having stirred up feelings
> thrill (*n.*)—a sudden feeling of excitement or strong emotion
> enjoyable (*adj.*)—being a source of pleasure or delight
> humorous (*adj.*)—funny, amusing
> pleasurable (*adj.*)—pleasant and agreeable

1. cheer/excited _____

_____

2. ride/thrill _____

_____

3. vacation/enjoyable _____

_____

4. comics/humorous _____

_____

5. weather/pleasurable _____

_____

Party Time!

These nouns are all things that may make you smile, laugh, or have fun. Read the nouns in the box below. Then fill in each line with the word from the box that best completes the sentence.

circus (*n.*)—a traveling show that has a variety of acts (such as acrobats, jugglers, clowns, and wild animal shows)
jokes (*n.*)—short stories with funny endings that lead to laughter
surprise (*n.*)—something that comes without warning
celebration (*n.*)—a festive gathering to mark a special event
carnival (*n.*)—a festival, often with rides and games

1. Rudi is the class clown. Luckily, our teacher likes his

   _____.

2. Michael's last birthday party was a _____.
   He thought we had forgotten!

3. Posters for the _____ show jugglers and tightrope
   walkers.

4. We will have a big _____ for Grandpa's sixtieth
   birthday.

5. I got my face painted at the _____ last week.

Daily Skill-Builders Vocabulary 4–5
walch.com © 2004 Walch Publishing

Fun Words

Clowning Around

Write a letter to a friend about a circus or carnival that you have seen.
Use at least five words from the box.

excited	enjoyable	pleasurable	jokes	celebration
thrill	humorous	circus	surprise	carnival

Dear _____,

_____

_____

_____

_____

_____

_____

_____

_____

_____

_____

_____

Yours Truly,

_____

Fun Words

All Mixed-Up

Unscramble each vocabulary word and write it on the short line. Then write the definition of the word on the long line.

1. risccu _____

_____

2. tecixde _____

_____

3. crlainav _____

_____

4. ejsko _____

_____

5. albupelsrea _____

_____

6. lhitrl _____

_____

7. pierusrs _____

_____

8. beyanojle _____

_____

9. eltiocebarn _____

_____

10. smoruhou _____

_____

Sad Times

Unfortunately, not all words describe happy times. There are words to describe other feelings, too. Here are some of them. Read the words in the box below. Then list two events that would cause each feeling.

lonely (*adj.*)—longing to be with other people
guilty (*adj.*)—feeling shameful for having done something wrong
worried (*adj.*)—feeling great concern
scared (*adj.*)—frightened or alarmed
angry (*adj.*)—feeling displeasure; upset or mad

1. lonely _____

_____

2. guilty _____

_____

3. worried _____

_____

4. scared _____

_____

5. angry _____

_____

Sad Words

A Painful Part

Pain and loss are a part of life. These nouns all have to do with the harder times in life. Read the nouns in the box below. Then fill in each line with the word from the box that best completes the sentence.

> sickness (*n.*)—illness; disease; poor health
> injury (*n.*)—damage suffered
> distress (*n.*)—pain or suffering in the mind or body
> loss (*n.*)—harm or distress that comes from losing something
> sadness (*n.*)—unhappiness

1. I have been feeling a sense of _____ since my dog ran away.

2. The team felt great _____ at the end of their last game.

3. Stella's _____ kept her out of basketball for a week.

4. The school closed for three days to stop the spread of a(n) _____ .

5. Her messy hair and chewed fingernails showed her _____ .

Painful Puzzle

Match each clue with a vocabulary word from the box. Write the vocabulary word in the puzzle.

angry	guilt	lonely	sadness	sickness
distress	injury	loss	scared	worried

Across

2. longing to be with other people
6. feeling displeasure; upset
7. illness; disease; poor health
9. pain or suffering of the mind or body
10. feeling great concern

Down

1. damage suffered
3. harm or distress that comes from losing something
4. unhappiness
5. a feeling of shame for having done something wrong
8. frightened

Sad Words

Pairing Off

Write a sentence using each word pair.

1. older/lonely _____

   _____

2. wrong/guilty _____

   _____

3. mother/worried _____

   _____

4. child/scared _____

   _____

5. feeling/angry _____

   _____

6. fever/sickness _____

   _____

7. sports/injury _____

   _____

8. hospital/distress _____

   _____

9. empty/loss _____

   _____

10. tears/sadness _____

   _____

Be Nice!

These adjectives have to do with being nice. Read the adjectives in the box below. Then name one person that each word describes. Write a sentence telling why you chose that person.

> helpful (*adj.*)—giving aid or relief to someone
> caring (*adj.*)—having concern or worry for another
> generous (*adj.*)—free in giving or sharing
> sincere (*adj.*)—honest; meaning what one says
> compassionate (*adj.*)—having or showing pity for and a desire
>   to help another

1. helpful _____   _____

   _____

2. caring _____   _____

   _____

3. generous _____   _____

   _____

4. sincere _____   _____

   _____

5. compassionate _____   _____

   _____

Nice and Not-So-Nice Words

Not-so-Nice

These words describe some negative behavior or qualities. Read each word in the box below. Then fill in each line with the word from the box that best completes the sentence.

> selfish (*adj.*)—taking care of oneself without thought for others
> cruel (*adj.*)—ready to hurt others
> unfair (*adj.*)—not fair or honest
> teasing (*v.*)—making fun of or annoying repeatedly
> greedy (*adj.*)—trying to grab or get more than one's share

1. Brian thought it was _____ of Jeff not to share his games.

2. The _____ boy took all the snacks for himself.

3. My brother won't stop _____ me about my new glasses.

4. I thought it was _____ that my brother and I were both sent to our rooms. He started it!

5. It is against the law to be _____ to animals.

Nice and Not-So-Nice Words

Help or Harm?

Match each clue with a vocabulary word from the box. Write the vocabulary word in the puzzle.

caring	cruel	greedy	selfish	teasing
compassionate	generous	helpful	sincere	unfair

Across

2. having concern or worry for another
3. giving aid or relief to someone
6. taking care of oneself without thought for others
8. free in giving or sharing
9. making fun of or annoying repeatedly

Down

1. having or showing pity for and a desire to help another
2. ready to hurt others
4. honest; meaning what one says
5. trying to grab more than one's share
7. not fair or honest

Nice and Not-So-Nice Words

Looking for Help

Write the definition of each vocabulary word. Then circle each vocabulary word in the word search. Words appear across, down, or diagonally.

1. helpful _____

2. selfish _____

3. caring _____

4. cruel _____

5. generous _____

6. unfair _____

7. sincere _____

8. teasing _____

9. compassionate _____

10. greedy _____

```
C I N G Y T E A S I N G R A T
H E L P F U L A I L M E N H S
U R C L E Z G U N F A I R E R
G E N A E C O M C E I J G L E
R E S P R I N G E E A T E P E
E R N A I I S S R O M Y C J F
E S P E C P N E E O U S R U D
D Y E W R L S G D I N G U L L
Y G O L L O S E C S P R E P Y
I N G T F I U E N S A T L E G
L T A T E I C S L Y T O U S O
C A T N F I S H T U E L C O N
G R R A N D A H N O U S R G X
D G P T R Y R A N F T F A R Y
C O M P A S S I O N A T E R E
```

Daily Skill-Builders Vocabulary 4–5
walch.com © 2004 Walch Publishing

Nice and Not-So-Nice Words

Words Behaving Badly

These words are about bad behavior. Read the words in the box below. Then fill in each line with the word from the box that best completes the sentence.

> cheating (*v.*)—using dishonest methods to gain an unfair
> advantage
> harm (*v.*)—to cause injury or hurt
> disrespect (*n.*)—lack of respect or poor attitude toward
> someone or something
> dishonest (*adj.*)—not trustworthy
> stealing (*v.*)—taking something that belongs to someone else

1. _____ on a test is unfair to those who studied.

2. Be careful not to _____ the puppy when you punish it.

3. It was _____ to ask for money for a fake charity.

4. Sitting during the national anthem is a sign of _____.

5. She could go to jail for _____ that watch!

Staying Safe

These words are about keeping safe and staying out of trouble. Read the words in the box below. Then fill in each line with the word from the box that best completes the sentence.

> rule (*n.*)—a guide or principle for behavior or action
> limit (*n.*)—a point beyond which a person or thing cannot go
> boundary (*n.*)—a dividing line that points out or shows an end
> shun (*v.*)—to keep away from
> obey (*v.*)—to follow the commands or guidance of

1. The _____ seemed strict, but it was for the best.

2. The _____ between the school grounds and the woods was clearly marked.

3. Wendi reached the _____ of allowed sick days early in the school year.

4. You should _____ situations that will lead to trouble.

5. He will _____ so he will not get scolded.

Wisdom of the Ages

In many cultures, elders, or older people, are highly respected. Why do you think this is? How do you feel about your elders? Explain your ideas using at least five words from the box.

| stealing | harm | dishonest | limit | shun |
| cheating | disrespect | rule | boundary | obey |

_____

_____

_____

_____

_____

_____

_____

_____

_____

_____

Behavior Words

Your Own World

Imagine you could make the rules for a brand new society. What things would be most important? How would you keep people safe and happy? Create eight major rules for your society. Use a vocabulary word from the box in each rule. Explain each rule.

stealing	harm	dishonest	limit	shun
cheating	disrespect	rule	boundary	obey

1. _____

_____

2. _____

_____

3. _____

_____

4. _____

_____

5. _____

_____

6. _____

_____

7. _____

_____

8. _____

_____

Behavior Words

Let's Talk

People communicate and make their feelings known in different ways. These verbs are about communication. Read the verbs in the box below. Then fill in each line with the word from the box that best completes the sentence.

> agree (v.)—to have the same opinion
> respond (v.)—to say something in return; to reply
> ignore (v.)—to pay no attention to
> discuss (v.)—to talk about something fully and openly
> complain (v.)—to express grief, pain, or discontent

1. Why must you _____ about every little thing that goes wrong?

2. We should _____ to the invitation before it is too late.

3. Sam tries to _____ her brother when he teases her.

4. We cannot buy the paint until we _____ on a color.

5. Read the chapter for homework, and we will _____ it in class tomorrow.

Talk It Out

These verbs are about interaction and communication. Read the verbs in the box below. Then write a sentence using each word pair.

> educate (*v.*)—to teach; to develop the mind and morals with
>   formal instruction
> assist (*v.*)—to give aid or help
> demonstrate (*v.*)—to explain or show clearly
> suggest (*v.*)—to offer as an idea
> listening (*v.*)—paying attention in order to hear

1. educate/books _____

   _____

2. assist/need _____

   _____

3. demonstrate/learn _____

   _____

4. suggest/effort _____

   _____

5. listening/care _____

   _____

Daily Skill-Builders Vocabulary 4–5
walch.com © 2004 Walch Publishing   Communication and Interaction

Some Good Advice

Imagine you have a friend who has a problem. Write a letter giving some advice. Use at least five words from the box.

agree	ignore	complain	assist	suggest
respond	discuss	educate	demonstrate	listening

Dear _____,

_____

_____

_____

_____

_____

_____

_____

_____

_____

_____

_____

Your Friend,

_____

Communication and Interaction

And the Letter Is . . .

Below are vocabulary words and definitions. Find the definition of each vocabulary word. Write the letter of the correct definition on the line.

1. _____ agree   **a.** to talk about something fully and openly

2. _____ respond   **b.** to offer as an idea

3. _____ ignore   **c.** to give aid or help

4. _____ discuss   **d.** to have the same opinion

5. _____ complain   **e.** paying attention in order to hear

6. _____ educate   **f.** to explain or show clearly

7. _____ assist   **g.** to pay no attention to

8. _____ demonstrate   **h.** to teach; to develop the mind and morals with formal instruction

9. _____ suggest   **i.** to say something in return; to reply

10. _____ listening   **j.** to express grief, pain, or discontent

Communication and Interaction

Look and See

There are many ways to look at something. These verbs are about looking at things. Read the verbs in the box below. Then write a sentence using each word.

stare (*v.*)—to look at long and hard, often with wide-open eyes
peek (*v.*)—to take a short, sly look, often through an opening
gaze (*v.*)—to take a long, steady look
search (*v.*)—to go through carefully and thoroughly in an effort
to find something
glance (*v.*)—to give a quick look

1. stare_____

_____

2. peek_____

_____

3. gaze _____

_____

4. search _____

_____

5. glance _____

_____

Vision Words

Seeing Is Believing

These nouns are all about seeing. Read the nouns in the box below. Then list two things you might see using each item. For *vision*, write what you see well with the naked eye.

---

vision (*n.*)—the act or power of seeing

eyeglasses (*n.*)—a pair of glass lenses set in a frame and worn in front of the eyes used to help one see better or clearly

binoculars (*n.*)—a handheld tool of two lenses for seeing at a distance

telescope (*n.*)—an instrument shaped like a long tube that has lenses for viewing objects at a great distance, especially for observing objects in space

video (*n.*)—the reception or transmission of television images

---

1. vision _____ _____

2. eyeglasses _____ _____

3. binoculars _____ _____

4. telescope _____ _____

5. video _____ _____

A Starting Point

People have used language to communicate for thousands of years. Over time, words and languages change. Sometimes, earlier forms of a word or related words can help us better understand a word.

The history of a word is its **origin.** In the dictionary, word origins may be listed after the word, usually in brackets.

origin (*n.*) [ME *origine,* probably from Middle French (MF), from Latin (L) *origin-, origo,* from *oriri* to rise, akin to Sanskrit (Skt) *rnoti* he moves, arises, from Greek (Gk) *ornynai* to rouse, *oros* mountain]

The languages Middle French, Latin, Sanskrit, and Greek are listed in order from newest to oldest, tracing a word back as far as it is known. In the example, you see that the word *origin* has been through many forms. It is related (akin) to a word meaning "he arises."

Match the origins below with one of the vocabulary words in the box. Write the vocabulary word on the line. One origin has two words.

search	stare	telescope	video	vision

1. from Gk *tele* far off and *skopos* watcher, related to Gk *skopein* to watch

   _____

2. related to Gk *stereo* solid and Lithuanian (Lith) *starinti* to stiffen

   _____

3. from L *videre* to see _____

4. probably from ME *cerchen* from MF *cerchier* to go about, from Late L *circare* to go about, from L *circum* round _____

Vision Words

Looking Good

Below are vocabulary words and definitions. Find the definition of each vocabulary word. Write the letter of the correct definition on the line.

1. _____ binoculars

2. _____ eyeglasses

3. _____ gaze

4. _____ glance

5. _____ peek

6. _____ search

7. _____ stare

8. _____ telescope

9. _____ video

10. _____ vision

a. the reception or transmission of television images

b. an instrument for viewing objects at a great distance

c. a handheld tool of two lenses for seeing at a distance

d. the act or power of seeing

e. to take a long, steady look

f. to give a quick look

g. a pair of glass lenses set in a frame and worn over the eyes used to help one see better

h. to look long and hard, with wide-open eyes

i. to go through carefully to find something

j. to take a short, sly look, often through an opening

Daily Skill-Builders Vocabulary 4–5
walch.com © 2004 Walch Publishing

Vision Words

All Shook Up!

These adjectives describe feelings that are not calm and peaceful. Read the adjectives in the box below. Then write a synonym and an antonym for each word.

> eager (*adj.*)—desiring very much; impatient
> anxious (*adj.*)—afraid about what might happen
> uncertain (*adj.*)—unsure
> doubtful (*adj.*)—not certain in outcome or result
> nervous (*adj.*)—easily excited or upset

	Synonym	**Antonym**
1. eager	_____	_____
2. anxious	_____	_____
3. uncertain	_____	_____
4. doubtful	_____	_____
5. nervous	_____	_____

Now use two of the words above in sentences of your own.

_____

_____

_____

_____

Tense Words

Scary Vocabulary!

These words all have to do with feeling fear. Read the words in the box below, if you dare! Then write a sentence using each word pair.

frightened (*adj.*)—very afraid or alarmed

horror (*n.*)—a great and painful fear, dread, or shock

terrified (*adj.*)—extremely afraid

panic (*n.*)—sudden, intense, overwhelming fear, often affecting a
whole group at once

fearful (*adj.*)—filled with a strong, unpleasant feeling caused by a sense
of danger or expecting something bad to happen

1. frightened/child _____

_____

2. horror/sight _____

_____

3. terrified/scream _____

_____

4. panic/dark _____

_____

5. fearful/shadows _____

_____

Worry Words

Match each clue with a vocabulary word from the box. Write the vocabulary word in the puzzle.

eager	uncertain	nervous	horror	panic
anxious	doubtful	frightened	terrified	fearful

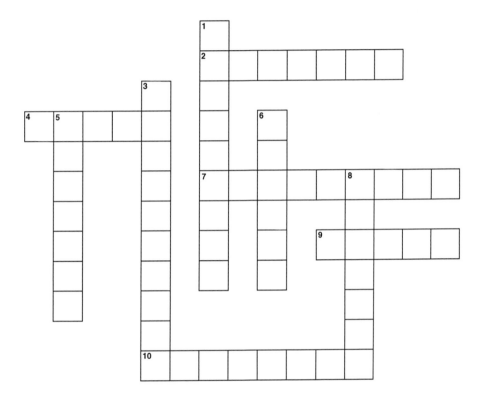

Across

2. easily excited or upset
4. desiring very much; impatient
7. extremely afraid
9. sudden, intense, overwhelming fear, often affecting a whole group at once
10. not certain in outcome or result

Down

1. unsure
3. very afraid or alarmed
5. afraid about what might happen
6. a great and painful fear, dread, or shock
8. filled with a strong unpleasant feeling caused by a sense of danger

Tense Words

Worried or Scared?

Explain the difference in meaning between the words in each pair.

1. panic/horror _____

_____

2. nervous/frightened _____

_____

3. fearful/doubtful _____

_____

4. terrified/anxious _____

_____

5. uncertain/eager _____

_____

Now use two vocabulary words in sentences of your own.

_____

_____

_____

_____

Tense Words

Unit 4 Review

A. Circle the letter of the word that does not belong. On the line, tell why that word does not belong.

1. **a.** cheating   **b.** stealing   **c.** greedy   **d.** helpful

_____

2. **a.** horror   **b.** eager   **c.** panic   **d.** terrified

_____

3. **a.** helpful   **b.** assist   **c.** compassionate   **d.** cruel

_____

4. **a.** eyeglasses   **b.** binoculars   **c.** telescope   **d.** vision

_____

5. **a.** celebration   **b.** circus   **c.** carnival   **d.** boundary

_____

B. Write a synonym for each vocabulary word.

1. scared   _____

2. uncertain   _____

3. excited   _____

4. humorous   _____

5. sickness   _____

Unit 4 Review, cont.

C. Choose an antonym from the box for each word. Write the correct antonym on the line.

| dishonest | painful | fair | happiness | sure |

1. doubtful _____

2. sadness _____

3. unfair _____

4. sincere _____

5. pleasurable _____

D. Below are vocabulary words and definitions. Find the definition of each vocabulary word. Write the letter of the correct definition on the line.

1. _____ shun   **a.** to explain or show clearly

2. _____ demonstrate   **b.** to keep away from

3. _____ gaze   **c.** to follow the commands or guidance of

4. _____ educate   **d.** to teach

5. _____ obey   **e.** to take a long, steady look

Transportation Time

There are many ways to travel from place to place. These nouns name types of transportation. Read the nouns in the box below. Then write a sentence using each word.

vehicle (n.)—something used to transport people or goods

automobile (n.)—a vehicle with four wheels that runs on its own power and carries passengers

taxi (n.)—a vehicle that carries passengers for a price set by the time and distance of the ride

motorcycle (n.)—a vehicle for one or two passengers that has two wheels and runs with a motor

scooter (n.)—a vehicle with a narrow base between a back wheel and a front wheel with a long handle attached to it

1. vehicle _____

_____

2. automobile _____

_____

3. taxi _____

_____

4. motorcycle _____

_____

5. scooter _____

_____

Transportation Words

Carrier Choices

How will you get where you want to go? Here are more nouns about transportation. Read the nouns in the box below. Then fill in each line with the word from the box that best completes the sentence.

> **airline** (*n.*)—a company or system of transportation by aircraft
>
> **helicopter** (*n.*)—an aircraft that flies using a rotating blade attached to its roof
>
> **ski lift** (*n.*)—a power-driven, continuously-moving belt that carries hanging chairs with skiers to the top of a mountain
>
> **rocket** (*n.*)—a jet engine used to propel a vehicle
>
> **space shuttle** (*n.*)—a spacecraft designed to transport people and cargo between Earth and space

1. Riding the _____ is much quicker than hiking up the mountain.

2. The instruments aboard the _____ read that they were about to reach the moon's orbit.

3. The _____ had enough power to shoot the spacecraft into space.

4. I like flying with this _____. They have the best movies!

5. The traffic reporter from the news station could look down on the highway from her _____.

Transportation Words

Any Letters for Me?

Read each definition. In the spaces, write the letters of the correct vocabulary word from the box.

vehicle	taxi	scooter	helicopter	rocket
automobile	motorcycle	airline	ski lift	space shuttle

1. a vehicle that carries passengers for a price
   — — — —

2. a company or system of transportation by aircraft
   — — — — — — —

3. a power-driven belt that carries skiers up a mountain
   — — — — — — —

4. a vehicle with a narrow base between a back wheel and a front wheel with a long handle
   — — — — — — —

5. a vehicle with four wheels that runs on its own power and carries passengers
   — — — — — — — — — —

6. a craft designed to transport people and cargo between Earth and space
   — — — — — — — — — — — —

7. an aircraft that flies using a rotating blade on its roof
   — — — — — — — — — —

8. a vehicle that has two wheels and runs with a motor
   — — — — — — — — — —

9. a jet engine used to propel a vehicle
   — — — — — —

10. something used to transport people or goods
    — — — — — — —

Transportation Words

Wish You Were Here!

Imagine you are on an amazing vacation—anywhere! Write a letter to a friend and tell where you have been and all the ways you have traveled. Use at least six words from the box.

vehicle	taxi	scooter	helicopter	rocket
automobile	motorcycle	airline	ski lift	space shuttle

Dear _____,

_____

_____

_____

_____

_____

_____

Your Friend,

_____

Daily Skill-Builders Vocabulary 4–5
walch.com © 2004 Walch Publishing

Transportation Words

One if by Land

These words all describe different types of land transportation. Read the words in the box below. Then fill in each line with the word from the box that best completes the sentence.

horseback (*adv.*)—on the back of a horse

carriage (*n.*)—a vehicle with wheels, and usually no motor, that carries people

bicycle (*n.*)—a vehicle having two wheels, one behind the other, that is usually moved by pedals

wagon (*n.*)—a vehicle with four wheels, and usually no motor, used for carrying goods

tricycle (*n.*)—a vehicle with three wheels that is usually moved by pedals

1. The small child was safer on the _____, because it was more stable with three wheels.

2. The riders were all on _____ as they entered the arena for the competition.

3. The couple took a quiet ride on a horse-drawn _____ around the city on their anniversary.

4. As they loaded up the _____, they realized that they would have to make another trip to carry everything they had.

5. Henry put special tires and shocks on his _____ so he could go over lots of jumps.

More Transportation Words

Two if by Sea

These nouns name forms of transportation designed for water travel. Read the nouns in the box below. Then write a sentence using each word pair.

> motorboat (*n.*)—an often small boat driven by a machine powered by gas or electricity
>
> yacht (*n.*)—a small ship used for pleasure cruising or racing
>
> submarine (*n.*)—a naval ship designed to operate underwater
>
> surfboard (*n.*)—a long, narrow board that floats and is ridden in surfing
>
> rowboat (*n.*)—a boat made to be rowed with oars or paddles

1. waves/motorboat _____

   _____

2. luxury/yacht _____

   _____

3. battle/submarine _____

   _____

4. ocean/surfboard _____

   _____

5. fish/rowboat _____

   _____

More Transportation Words

Mixed-Up Travel

Unscramble each vocabulary word, and write it on the short line. Then write the definition of the word on the long line.

1. asdorfrub _____

   _____

2. anogw _____

   _____

3. borcaheks _____

   _____

4. thayc _____

   _____

5. troomtabo _____

   _____

6. cetlryic _____

   _____

7. awrootb _____

   _____

8. rsebnamui _____

   _____

9. ceblciy _____

   _____

10. graceria _____

   _____

More Transportation Words

By Land or by Sea?

Match each clue with a vocabulary word from the box. Write the vocabulary word in the puzzle.

| horseback | bicycle | tricycle | yacht | surfboard |
| carriage | wagon | motorboat | submarine | rowboat |

Across
2. a vehicle with two wheels that is usually moved by pedals
5. a vehicle with wheels, and usually no motor, that carries people
8. a boat made to be moved with oars or paddles
9. a vehicle with three wheels that is usually moved by pedals
10. a naval ship designed to operate underwater

Down
1. a long, narrow board that floats and is ridden in surfing
3. a small ship used for pleasure cruising or racing
4. a vehicle with four wheels, and usually no motor, used for carrying goods
6. an often small boat driven by a machine powered by gas or electricity
7. on the back of a horse

More Transportation Words

Water, Water Everywhere

These words all have to do with water. Some describe small amounts, and others describe too much water! Read the words in the box below. Then fill in each line with the word from the box that best completes the sentence.

> rainwater (*n.*)—water falling or that has fallen as rain
> humid (*adj.*)—moist; damp
> moisture (*n.*)—a small amount of liquid that causes
>   something to be slightly wet
> flooded (*adj.*)—covered, filled with, or overtaken by
>   a huge flow of water
> drench (*v.*)—to wet or soak thoroughly

1. We collect _____ in a barrel and use it on the garden.

2. It was _____ in the locker room after everyone had showered.

3. The _____ clouded the mirrors.

4. The rain will _____ you if you go out now.

5. After the heavy rain, the ground floor apartment was _____.

Weather Words

You're All Wet

These nouns name things people use to deal with the rain. Read the nouns in the box below. Then write a sentence using each word.

umbrella (*n.*)—a fabric covering stretched over folding ribs attached
    to a rod or pole and used for protection usually against
    rain or sun

raincoat (*n.*)—a coat made of waterproof material to keep a person dry

forecast (*n.*)—a prediction of something in the future, often the
    coming weather

wipers (*n.*)—mechanical arms with a rubber edge that cleans, clears,
    or dries a surface, like a car's windshield, of water or rain

towels (*n.*)—cloths or pieces of absorbent paper for wiping or drying

1. umbrella _____

_____

2. raincoat _____

_____

3. forecast _____

_____

4. wipers _____

_____

5. towels _____

_____

Daily Skill-Builders Vocabulary 4–5
walch.com © 2004 Walch Publishing

Weather Words

Mopping Up with Metaphors

Like a simile, a **metaphor** compares two things. Unlike a simile, a metaphor does not use the word *like* or *as*. Here is an example of each.

> **Examples:** Jo is *as* tall *as* a telephone pole. **(simile)**
> Jo is a telephone pole. **(metaphor)**

Write a metaphor for five words that you choose from the box.

drench	forecast	moisture	rainwater	umbrella
flooded	humid	raincoat	towels	wipers

1. _____

_____

2. _____

_____

3. _____

_____

4. _____

_____

5. _____

_____

Weather Words

Weather on the Way!

Imagine that you are a weather forecaster. Write the forecast for next week. Be sure to use at least five of the words from the box. Feel free to add your own weather words as well!

rainwater	moisture	drench	raincoat	wipers
humid	flooded	umbrella	forecast	towels

Forecast for the week of _____

_____

_____

_____

_____

_____

_____

_____

_____

_____

_____

_____

_____

_____

_____

_____

_____

_____

Daily Skill-Builders Vocabulary 4–5
walch.com © 2004 Walch Publishing

Weather Words

Brrr . . .

These words all have to do with cold weather. Read the words in the box below. Then order the weather conditions from mildest to most severe.

> snowy (*adj.*)—having or covered with snow, small, white crystals of ice
>
> hail (*n.*)—small lumps of ice that fall from the clouds, sometimes during thunderstorms
>
> frigid (*adj.*)—freezing cold
>
> frost (*n.*)—a covering of tiny ice crystals on a cold surface formed from water vapor in the air
>
> blizzard (*n.*)—a long, heavy snowstorm

mildest

_____

_____

_____

_____

_____

most severe

More Weather Words

Storm Front

These nouns all have to do with different types of wind and weather. Read the nouns in the box below. Then write a sentence using each word pair.

> breeze (*n.*)—a gentle wind
> hurricane (*n.*)—a tropical cyclone with intense winds, usually with
> rain, thunder, and lightning
> tornado (*n.*)—a violent, whirling wind accompanied by a cloud
> that is shaped like a funnel and moves over land
> in a narrow path
> gale (*n.*)—a strong wind
> sleet (*n.*)—frozen or partly frozen rain

1. breeze/relax _____

_____

2. hurricane/danger _____

_____

3. tornado/warning _____

_____

4. gale/tumble _____

_____

5. sleet/numb _____

_____

More Weather Words

Puzzling Weather

Write the definition of each vocabulary word. Then circle each vocabulary word in the word search. Words appear across, down, or diagonally.

1. blizzard _____

2. breeze _____

3. frigid_____

4. frost _____

5. gale_____

6. hail_____

7. hurricane _____

8. sleet _____

9. snowy _____

10. tornado _____

```
E  S  N  O  W  Y  E  Z  O  W  S  I  F  F  T
A  S  H  E  B  R  E  E  Z  E  S  L  E  E  T
G  T  U  C  H  O  W  A  R  H  E  R  S  H  D
G  A  R  A  L  E  C  O  N  E  C  O  L  E  S
S  I  R  T  I  N  G  I  R  L  T  I  L  E  Z
T  O  I  A  R  Y  Z  A  L  E  Y  O  S  T  Z
Z  Z  C  T  O  P  S  B  L  I  Z  Z  A  R  D
H  E  A  G  O  T  C  K  E  E  C  H  R  S  T
I  L  N  R  C  K  N  M  F  I  A  F  F  R  D
R  R  E  H  U  R  Z  Z  F  R  Y  Q  R  Z  U
F  R  I  G  I  D  T  O  R  N  A  D  O  R  M
D  Y  Z  H  C  K  S  T  N  M  A  Z  S  Y  A
K  A  V  N  H  A  I  L  M  A  T  E  T  R  I
Z  R  I  N  G  A  R  D  S  T  A  R  T  E  R
O  R  A  R  D  A  B  E  C  I  D  O  E  U  Y
```

More Weather Words

Which Weather?

Below are vocabulary words and definitions. Find the definition of each vocabulary word. Write the letter of the correct definition on the line.

1. _____ snowy

2. _____ hail

3. _____ frigid

4. _____ frost

5. _____ blizzard

6. _____ breeze

7. _____ hurricane

8. _____ tornado

9. _____ gale

10. _____ sleet

a. small lumps of ice that fall from the clouds, sometimes during thunderstorms

b. a violent, whirling wind accompanied by a cloud that is shaped like a funnel and moves in a narrow path

c. a covering of tiny ice crystals on a cold surface formed from water vapor in the air

d. frozen or partly frozen rain

e. having or covered with snow, small, white crystals of ice

f. a tropical cyclone with intense winds, usually with rain, thunder, and lightning

g. freezing cold

h. a long, heavy snowstorm

i. a gentle wind

j. a strong wind

More Weather Words

We Have a Problem!

Bad weather is not the only problem we may face. These words are about other problems. Read the words in the box below. Then write a sentence using each word.

> disease (*n.*)—an illness or change in a living thing that keeps it from functioning normally
>
> accident (*n.*)—something bad that happens by chance
>
> enemies (*n.*)—people who hate, attack, or try to harm someone
>
> embarrass (*v.*)—to cause to feel confused, distressed, and uncomfortable
>
> odor (*n.*)—a smell, whether pleasant or unpleasant

1. disease _____

_____

2. accident _____

_____

3. enemies _____

_____

4. embarrass _____

_____

5. odor _____

_____

Something Gone Bad

These words all have to do with something breaking down. Read the words in the box below. Then write a sentence using each word pair.

ruined (*adj.*)—damaged or destroyed beyond repair; cannot be fixed
error (*n.*)—a mistake
spoil (*v.*)—to decay or lose freshness, value, or usefulness by being kept too long
rust (*n.*)—a reddish coating formed on metal when it is exposed to moist air for some time
malfunction (*n.*)—a failure to serve a certain purpose or work properly

1. ruined/building _____

   _____

2. error/homework _____

   _____

3. spoil/milk _____

   _____

4. rust/bike _____

   _____

5. malfunction/computer _____

   _____

Daily Skill-Builders Vocabulary 4–5
walch.com © 2004 Walch Publishing

Problem Words

Poor Rusty

Write a short story about a boy or girl named Rusty who is having a terrible day. Use at least six of the words from the box.

disease	enemies	odor	error	rust
accident	embarrass	ruined	spoil	malfunction

_____

(title)

_____

_____

_____

_____

_____

_____

_____

_____

_____

_____

Problem Words

Looking for Trouble

Write the definition of each vocabulary word. Then circle each vocabulary word in the word search. Words appear across, down, or diagonally.

1. disease _____

2. ruined _____

3. accident _____

4. error _____

5. enemies _____

6. spoil _____

7. embarrass _____

8. rust _____

9. odor _____

10. malfunction _____

```
A O D O R I F I C A L O U S E
R C F R I E N D E N E M I E S
S D C E R R O R M R U I N E D
P A E I I R R I B M O M F T C
O D O C D P I M A M P A N D R
I O I C I E D E R C A L O E A
L R R S U O N S R C C F S N I
E O P Y E U O T A I N U D T O
C C O M M A R T S R R N S S R
C I A D O S S Y S S O C D S E
A A Y E D E M E M I S T A K E
F I X N R R S I I R R I N A I
D P A T Y A D S R E P O I L R
A O S Y S O S O A S G N O Y R
R R A D N D E N T C C R U S T
```

Daily Skill-Builders Vocabulary 4–5
walch.com © 2004 Walch Publishing

Problem Words

Fix It Up!

These words all have to do with solving problems. Read the words in the box below. Then write a sentence using each word.

repair (*v.*)—to fix; to put back into good condition
replace (*v.*)—to put something new in the place of something else
correct (*v.*)—to make or set right
solution (*n.*)—the answer; the result of solving a problem
discover (*v.*)—to find out, especially for the first time

1. repair_____

_____

2. replace_____

_____

3. correct_____

_____

4. solution_____

_____

5. discover_____

_____

Make Your Case

These words all have to do with proving a point. Read the words in the box below. Then fill in each line with the word from the box that best completes the sentence.

> confirm (*v.*)—to remove doubt by giving facts
> logic (*n.*)—sound reasoning or common sense
> persist (*v.*)—to continue stubbornly
> reason (*n.*)—the power of thinking; intelligence
> rational (*adj.*)—relating to reason; showing understanding

1. I didn't need the instructions. A little _____ was the only tool I used.

2. If you _____ in talking during class, you will have to visit the principal.

3. The experiment will _____ our idea.

4. The only _____ explanation for failing is that you were tired that day.

5. Human beings' _____ is one trait that sets us apart from animals.

Problem Solving

Solving Words

Explain the relationship between the words in each pair.

1. repair/replace _____

   _____

2. discover/persist _____

   _____

3. confirm/rational _____

   _____

4. solution/correct_____

   _____

5. reason/logic_____

   _____

Fixer-Upper

Match each clue with a vocabulary word from the box. Write the vocabulary word in the puzzle.

confirm
correct
discover
logic
persist
rational
reason
repair
replace
solution

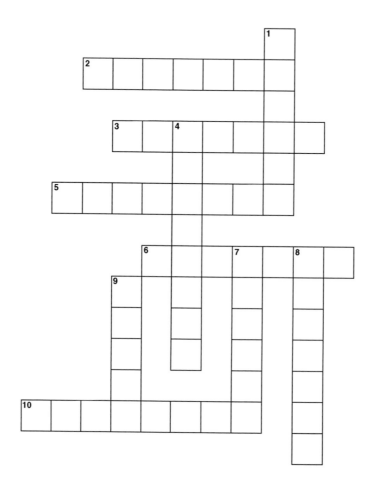

Across

2. to put something new in place of something else
3. to continue stubbornly
5. the answer; the result of solving a problem
6. to make or set right
10. to find out, especially for the first time

Down

1. the power of thinking; intelligence
4. relating to reason; showing understanding
7. to fix; to put back into good condition
8. to remove doubt by giving facts
9. sound reasoning; common sense

Constructive Work

The words in the box may apply to people who want to do well. Read the words in the box below. Then fill in each line with the word from the box that best completes the sentence.

instruction (*n.*)—a lesson; the practice of teaching
practice (*v.*)—to work at often, so as to learn to do well
advice (*n.*)—suggestions about a decision or an action
scholar (*n.*)—one who has done advanced study in a subject
desire (*n.*)—a strong wish or longing for something

1. The math _____ seemed to be able to do all the problems in her head.

2. Could you give me some _____ about a problem I'm having?

3. We need to _____ if we want to learn to do the dance steps by Friday.

4. It is my greatest _____ to learn to do stunts on my bike.

5. I'll need more _____ before I'll be able to do this word problem.

Teaching and Learning

Levels of Learning

There are many different levels of ability in all areas of learning and understanding. These words describe a person's level of ability. Read the words in the box below. Then write a sentence using each word pair.

> capable (*adj.*)—able to do one's job well
> clumsy (*adj.*)—lacking skill in grace or movement; badly or awkwardly done or made
> skillful (*adj.*)—having or showing an ability that comes from training or practice
> experienced (*adj.*)—made skillful or wise through practice or living through something
> master (*v.*)—to get control of or become very skilled at something

1. capable/task _____

   _____

2. clumsy/break _____

   _____

3. skillful/easy _____

   _____

4. experienced/time _____

   _____

5. master/level _____

   _____

Teaching and Learning

Sentence Completions

Below are ten sentence starters. Each contains a vocabulary word. Complete each sentence with information about yourself. Be sure to use the correct end punctuation.

1. I enjoy **instruction** in_____

2. I still need to **practice** my _____

3. I might become a **scholar** of _____

4. The strangest **advice** I received is _____

_____

5. Someday I have a **desire** to _____

6. I am fully **capable** of _____

7. I was **clumsy** when _____

8. I am rather **skillful** at _____

9. I am **experienced** in _____

10. With enough training, I can **master** _____

Puzzle Practice

Match each clue with a vocabulary word from the box. Write the vocabulary word in the puzzle.

| instruction | advice | desire | clumsy | experienced |
| practice | scholar | capable | skillful | master |

Across

1. suggestions about a decision
3. one who has done advanced study in a subject
4. a lesson or the practice of teaching
7. to get control of or become very skillful at something
8. to work at often, so as to do well
9. made skillful or wise through practice or living through something

Down

2. a strong wish or longing for something
3. having or showing an ability that comes from training or practice
5. lacking skill in grace or movement; badly or awkwardly done or made
6. able to do one's job well

Daily Skill-Builders Vocabulary 4–5
walch.com © 2004 Walch Publishing

Teaching and Learning

Unit 5 Review

A. Circle the letter of the word that does not belong. On the line, tell why that word does not belong.

1. **a.** carriage   **b.** helicopter   **c.** bicycle   **d.** wagon

_____

2. **a.** submarine   **b.** rowboat   **c.** yacht   **d.** ski lift

_____

3. **a.** logic   **b.** reason   **c.** rational   **d.** capable

_____

4. **a.** rainwater   **b.** odor   **c.** moisture   **d.** flooded

_____

5. **a.** frost   **b.** hurricane   **c.** tornado   **d.** gale

_____

B. In your own words, write the definition of each vocabulary word.

1. malfunction _____

2. persist _____

3. master _____

4. confirm _____

5. replace _____

Unit 5 Review, cont.

C. Below are vocabulary words and definitions. Find the definition of each vocabulary word. Write the letter of the correct definition on the line.

1. _____ logic   **a.** a smell

2. _____ desire   **b.** sound reasoning; common sense

3. _____ odor   **c.** a mistake

4. _____ solution   **d.** the answer; the result of solving a problem

5. _____ error   **e.** a strong wish or longing for something

D. Write a sentence using each word.

1. vehicle _____

2. discover _____

3. spoil _____

4. blizzard _____

5. skillful _____

E. Choose a synonym from the box for each vocabulary word. Write the correct synonym on the line.

cold	damp	fix	sickness	soak

1. repair _____

2. frigid _____

3. humid _____

4. drench _____

5. disease _____

Daily Skill-Builders Vocabulary 4–5
walch.com © 2004 Walch Publishing

Unit 5 Review

Bank On It!

These words all have to do with banking. Read the words in the box below.
Then write a sentence using each word pair.

> deposit (*v.*)—to put money into a bank
> withdraw (*v.*)—to take money out of a bank
> account (*n.*)—a record of money received, paid,
>   or taken out of the bank
> checking (*adj.*)—a type of account that allows a person
>   to write checks to pay for things
> savings (*adj.*)—a type of account into which money is
>   deposited and not taken out regularly

1. deposit/week _____

_____

2. withdraw/payment _____

_____

3. account/bank _____

_____

4. checking/bills _____

_____

5. savings/future _____

_____

Banking and Eating Words

Out to Lunch

These verbs all have to do with restaurants. Read the verbs in the box below. Then fill in each line with the word from the box that best completes the sentence.

> order (v.)—to tell what one wants to buy or eat, usually at a restaurant
> serve (v.)—to help people to food or to set out helpings of food or
>   drink, as a waiter or waitress
> prepare (v.)—to put together the elements of
> reserve (v.)—to arrange to have set aside and held for one's use
> deliver (v.)—to bring to an intended place

1. We should _____ a table at that restaurant.

2. I will _____ toast for breakfast.

3. The chef begins to _____ the meals long before
   the restaurant opens.

4. We looked at the new menu to decide what to
   _____.

5. Let's call the pizza place and have them _____
   lunch to Jena's.

Banking and Eating Words

Food Bank

Read each definition. In the spaces, write the letters of the correct vocabulary word from the box.

deposit	account	savings	serve	reserve
withdraw	checking	order	prepare	deliver

1. to put together the elements of a meal   _ _ _ _ _ _ _

2. a record of money received and taken out of a bank   _ _ _ _ _ _ _

3. to put money into a bank   _ _ _ _ _ _ _

4. to bring to an intended place   _ _ _ _ _ _ _

5. to tell what one wants to buy or eat for a meal   _ _ _ _ _

6. a type of account into which money is deposited and not taken out regularly   _ _ _ _ _ _ _

7. to arrange to have set aside and held for one's use   _ _ _ _ _ _ _

8. to take money out of a bank   _ _ _ _ _ _ _ _

9. to help people to food or set out helpings of food or drink, as a waiter or waitress   _ _ _ _ _

10. a type of account that allows a person to write checks to pay for things   _ _ _ _ _ _ _ _

Banking and Eating Words

Relating Words

Write a sentence using each word pair.

1. deposit/account _____

_____

2. checking/savings _____

_____

3. serve/order _____

_____

4. withdraw/deliver _____

_____

5. prepare/reserve _____

_____

Banking and Eating Words

Out to Eat

These nouns name places people can buy food. Read the nouns in the box below. Then write two things you might buy at each place.

bakery (*n.*)—a place where baked goods (cakes, breads, pastries) are sold

café (*n.*)—a small restaurant that sells coffee and casual food

cafeteria (*n.*)—a restaurant where people serve themselves

deli (*n.*)—a store that sells ready-to-eat foods, such as cooked meats and salads. Also called a *delicatessen*.

diner (*n.*)—a small restaurant that serves simple food, often at a counter. A diner usually looks like a railroad dining car in shape.

1. bakery _____ _____

2. café _____ _____

3. cafeteria _____ _____

4. deli _____ _____

5. diner _____ _____

Now use two of the words above in sentences of your own.

_____

_____

_____

_____

Shopping for Words

These nouns all have to do with going shopping. Read the nouns in the box below. Then write a sentence using each word.

> cart (*n.*)—a metal vehicle with four wheels used to carry
>   goods being bought or sold
> merchandise (*n.*)—goods that are bought and sold
> discount (*n.*)—an amount taken off a regular price
> value (*n.*)—something's worth in money or importance
> variety (*n.*)—a collection of different things

1. cart _____

_____

2. merchandise _____

_____

3. discount _____

_____

4. value _____

_____

5. variety _____

_____

Shopping and Eating Words

Shop Around

Below are vocabulary words and definitions. Find the definition of each vocabulary word. Write the letter of the correct definition on the line.

1. _____ deli

2. _____ café

3. _____ cafeteria

4. _____ bakery

5. _____ diner

6. _____ cart

7. _____ merchandise

8. _____ discount

9. _____ value

10. _____ variety

a. something's worth in money or importance

b. a place where baked goods are sold

c. a metal vehicle with four wheels used to carry goods being bought or sold

d. a small restaurant that sells coffee and casual food

e. a collection of different things

f. a store that sells ready-to-eat foods, such as cooked meats and salads

g. a small restaurant that serves simple food and looks like a dining car of a train

h. a restaurant where people serve themselves

i. goods that are bought and sold

j. an amount taken off a regular price

Shopping and Eating Words

Cheap Eats

Match each clue with a vocabulary word from the box. Write the vocabulary word in the puzzle.

bakery	cafeteria	deli	discount	value
café	cart	diner	merchandise	variety

Across

6. a restaurant where people serve themselves
7. a store where baked goods are sold
8. a small restaurant that looks like a dining car
9. a store that sells ready-to-eat foods, such as meats and salads
10. a collection of different things

Down

1. an amount taken off a regular price
2. a metal vehicle with four wheels used to carry goods
3. a small restaurant that serves coffee and casual food
4. goods that are bought and sold
5. something's worth in money or importance

Shopping and Eating Words

What's Your Role?

These nouns name roles of different people in a store. Read the nouns in the box below. Then fill in each line with the word from the box that best completes the sentence.

salesperson (*n.*)—a person who sells things in a store or door-to-door
security (*n.*)—a department or group of people who ensure safety for people and goods
customer (*n.*)—a person who buys from or uses the services of a company or store
custodian (*n.*)—a person who takes care of a certain place, often in the role of cleaning
cashier (*n.*)—a person who runs a register in a store and is responsible for money

1. When I finished all of my shopping, I paid the _____.

2. The _____ answered my questions about the DVD player.

3. I always feel safer when I see _____ in a store.

4. Each _____ received a discount just for shopping there today.

5. At the end of the day, the _____ will wash and polish the floors.

Shopping and Working Words

Shopping List

These verbs tell actions that take place in a store. Read the verbs in the box below. Then write a sentence using each word pair.

> select (*v.*)—to choose or pick out from a number or a group
> refund (*v.*)—to give back or repay, usually money
> purchase (*v.*)—to buy
> bargain (*v.*)—to discuss the terms of a purchase or agreement
> label (*v.*)—to attach a slip of paper to something to identify or describe it

1. select/ripe _____

_____

2. refund/broken _____

_____

3. purchase/best _____

_____

4. bargain/deal _____

_____

5. label/information _____

_____

Shopping and Working Words

Looking for a Bargain

Write the definition of each vocabulary word. Then circle each vocabulary word in the word search. Words appear across, down, or diagonally.

1. salesperson _____

2. select _____

3. security _____

4. refund _____

5. customer _____

6. purchase _____

7. custodian _____

8. bargain _____

9. cashier _____

10. label _____

```
B P U R P E T L I F E L O S S
A F U N D Y S E L E C T D E I
Y I M A C U S T O D I A N A T
O S A L T R A I R T E A R A T
F O U L B A L C U S T O M E R
D B R E Y F E U C H N B F C H
P U R C H A S E S G L G U Y L
C L H E C K P I E E A A T G R
G F Y C F S E A C A S E B Y I
C A S H I E R D U F D U N E T
C B I S G C S U R I T U M B L
B Y L A K E O F I R E F U N D
A D R I E R N Y T S E L E S T
B A R G A I N A Y C H P E R S
B O G R X F U N D A I N S O N
```

Shopping and Working Words

Suggestion Box

Imagine you have just visited a new store. Write a letter, politely telling the manager about your experience. Use at least six words from the box.

salesperson	customer	cashier	refund	bargain
security	custodian	select	purchase	label

Dear Manager,

_____

_____

_____

_____

_____

_____

_____

_____

_____

_____

Sincerely,

_____

Down to Business

These words are about business and work. Read the words in the box below.
Then write a sentence using each word pair.

> transaction (*n.*)—a business deal
> service (*n.*)—the work or action of someone who helps or is
> useful to others
> employ (*v.*)—to use the services of; to hire for pay or salary
> salary (*n.*)—a fixed or set amount of money paid at regular
> times for work done
> overtime (*n.*)—time spent working that is more than one usually
> works or is expected to work in a day or week

1. transaction/agree _____

_____

2. service/need _____

_____

3. employ/summer _____

_____

4. salary/year _____

_____

5. overtime/hours _____

_____

Doing Business

These words all have to do with the details of doing business. Read the words in the box below. Then fill in each line with the word from the box that best completes the sentence.

> damaged (*adj.*)—harmed due to injury
> competition (*n.*)—a contest
> schedule (*n.*)—a list of times set for something or someone
> delivery (*n.*)—the transfer of something from one place to another
> billing (*v.*)—the action of recording goods sold and asking for the
>   money owed for them

1. _____ for customers is fierce between the two bookstores.

2. I must check the _____ to see what hours I will be working next week.

3. The plumber will be _____ us for the hours it took to repair the faucet.

4. We are expecting a huge _____ of toys before the holiday sale.

5. This box of computer parts was dropped, and many of the items inside were _____.

Business Partners

Write a sentence using each word pair.

1. schedule/overtime_____

_____

2. competition/service _____

_____

3. transaction/delivery _____

_____

_____

4. employ/salary _____

_____

5. damaged/billing _____

_____

Business Terms

In your own words, write the definition of each vocabulary word.

1. transaction _____

_____

2. employ _____

_____

3. overtime _____

_____

4. competition _____

_____

5. delivery _____

_____

6. service _____

_____

7. salary _____

_____

8. damaged _____

_____

9. schedule _____

_____

10. billing _____

_____

To Your Benefit!

These words all have to do with the benefits that come from hard work, good character, and a good education. Read the words in the box below. Then explain how each word relates to hard work.

promotion (*n.*)—a rise in position or rank
future (*n.*)—time coming after the present; what has not happened yet
friendships (*n.*)—bonds with people whom one trusts and has a strong
                liking for
expertise (*n.*)—special skill or knowledge from training
contribute (*v.*)—to give along with others or share in something

1. promotion _____

_____

2. future _____

_____

3. friendships _____

_____

4. expertise _____

_____

5. contribute _____

_____

Great Results

Here are some more nouns that name some benefits of hard work and a good education. Read the nouns in the box below. Then fill in each line with the word from the box that best completes the sentence.

selection (*n.*)—a choice
housing (*n.*)—a place to live for a number of people
luxury (*n.*)—very rich, pleasant, and comfortable surroundings
vacations (*n.*)—periods of time spent away from home
or business in travel or amusement
respect (*n.*)—admiration and honor for someone

1. Because I received good grades, I have a wide _____ of jobs to choose from when I graduate.

2. Hard work has earned me the _____ of my teachers.

3. We have several _____ from school during the year.

4. We are now able to live a life of _____ thanks to hard work.

5. At college, my sister lives with a group of friends in student _____.

Benefit Words

Goals for Myself

Use each vocabulary word in a sentence about yourself.

1. promotion _____

   _____

2. future _____

   _____

3. friendships _____

   _____

4. expertise _____

   _____

5. contribute _____

   _____

6. selection _____

   _____

7. housing _____

   _____

8. luxury _____

   _____

9. vacations _____

   _____

10. respect _____

   _____

Priorities

A priority is something important that you put before something else. Write a paragraph about your five most important priorities for the future. Use at least five words from the box.

promotion	friendships	contribute	housing	vacations
future	expertise	selection	luxury	respect

_____

_____

_____

_____

_____

_____

_____

_____

_____

_____

_____

Benefit Words

In Office

These nouns name some of the leaders in our society. Read the nouns in the box below. Then write a sentence using each word pair.

> mayor (*n.*)—an official elected to serve as head of a city
>
> governor (*n.*)—an elected person who rules as the head of a state of the United States
>
> senator (*n.*)—a member of the smaller and upper branch of the legislature
>
> representative (*n.*)—a member of the larger branch of the legislature who acts for or in place of a group of people or county in one of the states of a democracy
>
> commissioner (*n.*)—an official who is the head of a governmental department

1. mayor/parade _____

_____

2. governor/conference _____

_____

3. senator/Washington D.C. _____

_____

4. representative/elect _____

_____

5. commissioner/oversee _____

_____

Passing Through

These nouns all have to do with rest and travel. Read the nouns in the box below. Then respond to each item in a complete sentence.

traveler (*n.*)—one who journeys from place to place or to a distant place

visitor (*n.*)—a person who makes a brief stay at a place not his or hers

passenger (*n.*)—someone riding on or in a vehicle

guest (*n.*)—a person entertained in someone else's home

acquaintance (*n.*)—a person one knows slightly, but not well

1. What are three places or things that a **traveler** might go to see in your town?_____

_____

2. Write a sentence that includes the word *visitor*. _____

_____

3. Where might someone be or have a **passenger?** _____

_____

4. List two things a **guest** should do when staying at someone's home. ____

_____

5. Name three places where you have made an **acquaintance.** _____

_____

Daily Skill-Builders Vocabulary 4–5
walch.com © 2004 Walch Publishing

Government and Travel

Who Is Who?

Below are vocabulary words and definitions. Find the definition of each vocabulary word. Write the letter of the correct definition on the line.

1. _____ mayor

2. _____ governor

3. _____ senator

4. _____ representative

5. _____ commissioner

6. _____ traveler

7. _____ visitor

8. _____ passenger

9. _____ guest

10. _____ acquaintance

a. an elected person who rules as the head of a state of the United States

b. an official who is the head of a governmental department

c. a person one knows slightly, but not well

d. an official elected to serve as head of a city

e. one who journeys from place to place or to a distant place

f. a person entertained in someone else's home

g. a member of the smaller and upper branch of the legislature

h. someone riding on or in a vehicle

i. a person who makes a brief stay at a place not his or hers

j. a member of the larger branch of the legislature who acts for or in place of a group of people or county in one of the states of a democracy

Government and Travel

Where's the Leader?

Match each clue with a vocabulary word from the box. Write the vocabulary word in the puzzle.

mayor	commissioner	senator	visitor	guest
governor	representative	traveler	passenger	acquaintance

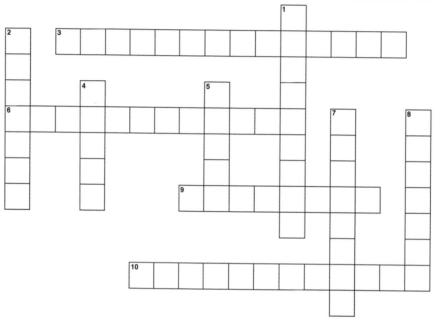

Across

3. a member of the larger branch of the legislature who acts in place of people in one of the states in a democracy
6. a person one knows slightly, not well
9. one who journeys from place to place
10. an official who is the head of a governmental department

Down

1. someone riding on or in a vehicle
2. a member of the smaller and upper branch of the legislature
4. a person entertained in someone else's home
5. an official elected to serve as head of a city
7. an elected person who rules as the head of a state
8. a person who makes a brief stay at a place not his or hers

 Daily Skill-Builders Vocabulary 4–5
walch.com © 2004 Walch Publishing   **Government and Travel**

Miles to Go

These words all have to do with traveling to learn or see something new.
Read the words in the box below. Then list two things each word makes you
think of.

journey (n.)—a long trip from one place to another
tour (n.)—a trip that ends at the point where it starts
        and shows people things along the way
explore (v.)—to go into or through for purposes of
        discovery or to find something new
pioneer (n.)—an early settler
roam (v.)—to go from place to place with no fixed or
        real purpose or direction

1. journey _____ _____

2. tour _____ _____

3. explore _____ _____

4. pioneer _____ _____

5. roam _____ _____

Use one word from above in a sentence of your own.

_____

_____

Journeys and Exploration

Travel Time

These nouns name what people can see or study when traveling. Read the nouns in the box below. Then write a sentence using each word pair.

---

past (*n.*)—time and events having occurred before the present; time gone by

museum (*n.*)—a building that displays objects of interest in one or more of the arts or sciences

knight (*n.*)—a warrior of medieval times who served a king, held a special military rank, fought on horseback, and behaved in a noble way

pyramid (*n.*)—a large structure built especially in ancient Egypt that usually has a square base and four triangular sides meeting at a point; contains tombs

tomb (*n.*)—a grave or burial chamber for dead people

---

1. past/learn _____

_____

2. museum/ancient _____

_____

3. knight/brave _____

_____

4. pyramid/stone _____

_____

5. tomb/sacred _____

_____

Journeys and Exploration

Seeing the Sites

Imagine that you have just taken a trip around the world. Write a letter to a friend describing the wonderful things you have seen on this trip. Use at least six of the words from the box.

journey	explore	roam	museum	pyramid
tour	pioneer	past	knight	tomb

Dear _____,

_____

_____

_____

_____

_____

_____

_____

_____

_____

_____

_____

Your Friend,

_____

Journeys and Exploration

Where Were We?

Unscramble each vocabulary word and write it on the short line. Then write the definition of the word on the long line.

1. dripamy   _____

_____

2. aspt   _____

_____

3. noepire   _____

_____

4. utor   _____

_____

5. hintgk   _____

_____

6. mtbo   _____

_____

7. roxpeel   _____

_____

8. ujenoyr   _____

_____

9. orma   _____

_____

10. emmuus   _____

_____

Unit 6 Review

A. Circle the letter of the word that does not belong. On the line, tell why that word does not belong.

1.   **a.** cashier   **b.** deposit   **c.** reserve   **d.** salary

_____

2.   **a.** journey   **b.** traveler   **c.** past   **d.** roam

_____

3.   **a.** acquaintance **b.** mayor   **c.** governor   **d.** senator

_____

4.   **a.** pyramid   **b.** knight   **c.** museum   **d.** tomb

_____

5.   **a.** label   **b.** discount   **c.** billing   **d.** refund

_____

B. Write a sentence using each word pair.

1. cafeteria/cashier _____

_____

2. variety/merchandise _____

_____

3. pioneer/explore _____

_____

4. promotion/savings _____

_____

5. vacations/luxury _____

_____

Unit 6 Review, cont.

C. Fill in each line with the word from the box that best completes the sentence.

custodian	expertise	respect	schedule	tour

1. He gained his _____ through many years at his job.

2. We all feel _____ for the woman who started this company.

3. The _____ of the museum ended before I saw the famous painting.

4. Please tell the _____ that there is a puddle on the floor.

5. His new _____ did not leave him much free time.

D. In your own words, write the definition of each vocabulary word.

1. cafeteria _____

2. housing _____

3. passenger _____

4. bargain _____

5. purchase _____

Answer Key

UNIT ONE

SCHOOL WORDS

Page 1: School Action
1. research
2. define
3. study
4. correct
5. outline

Page 2: Tools for Learning
Answers will vary.
1. atlas, Internet, questions, encyclopedia, dictionary
2. dictionary, questions, Internet
3. Internet
4. Internet, questions, encyclopedia
5. atlas, Internet, questions, encyclopedia

Page 3: School Sentences
Sample sentences:
1. I need to study for the English test.
2. We will define the words, and then we can understand what they mean.
3. The class will outline the information about Georgia.
4. When I take time to correct my mistakes, my grades improve.
5. Jane is curious to research the ancient writings.
6. Using a dictionary helps us learn words.
7. Before we travel, an atlas can show where and how far we are going.
8. Many times an encyclopedia will have the answers.
9. Dad searches the Internet to find good airfares.
10. It is wise to ask questions when the answers are not clear.

Page 4: School Match
1. c 2. e 3. b 4. g 5. i 6. h 7. a 8. j 9. d 10. f

PEOPLE AND PLACES AT SCHOOL

Page 5: People at School
Sample sentences:
1. The school counselor helps students to select appropriate courses.
2. Janitors keep the school neat and fix anything that breaks.
3. The principal was in charge of the fire drill.
4. We ask the secretary for a record of our grades.
5. My mom is a volunteer in the fifth-grade class.

Page 6: School Spaces
Answers will vary.

Page 7: Schoolwork
1. head of a school
2. where reference books are kept for use, not for sale
3. one who keeps records, letters, and does other office work in a school office
4. a room where classes meet
5. person who gives advice
6. large room or hall
7. person who takes care of a building
8. place where business is done
9. a person who helps without pay
10. a corridor that connects rooms in a building

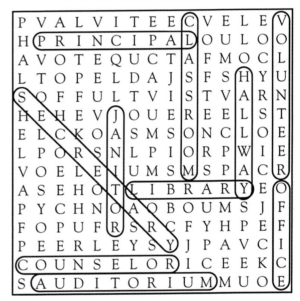

Page 8: School Similes
Sample similes:
1. Our principal is as wise as an owl.
2. The secretary is as watchful as a sentry.
3. My counselor is as happy as a clam.
4. Our janitor works like a horse.
5. Our reading volunteer is as kind as a saint.
6. The library in our school is as bright as a playhouse stage.
7. My art classroom is as busy as an ant farm.
8. The auditorium can be like a furnace in June.
9. The school office is like a busy intersection at rush hour.
10. Our hallway, displaying student drawings, is as attractive as an art gallery.

LEARNING WORDS

Page 9: Lots to Learn
Possible answers:
1. Europe; north; deserts
2. government; Civil War; Congress
3. add; algebra; geometry
4. test tubes; experiments; laboratory
5. spelling; reading; art

Page 10: Lots More to Learn
1. geology
2. anatomy
3. astronomy
4. chemistry
5. biology

Page 11: Space for Rent
1. science
2. astronomy
3. biology
4. geography
5. subject
6. chemistry
7. mathematics
8. geology
9. anatomy
10. history

Page 12: A Letter Home
Letters will vary.

GRAMMAR AND WRITING WORDS

Page 13: Tools of the Trade
Answers will vary.

Page 14: Write Away!
1. application
2. composition
3. sentence
4. form
5. paragraph

Page 15: In Your Own Words
Answers will vary.

Page 16: Caution: Words Crossing!

MATH WORDS

Page 17: Number Sense?
1. dividend
2. sum
3. quotient
4. product
5. divisor

Page 18: More Math
1. width
2. height
3. total
4. difference
5. altogether

Page 19: Sentenced to Math
1. height
2. dividend
3. product
4. difference
5. total, altogether, sum
6. width
7. divisor
8. quotient

Page 20: Does It Add Up?
Sample sentences:
1. You can find the sum by adding.
2. The test question asked me to find the product of two numbers.
3. The answer to a division problem is a quotient.
4. The number of the divisor is too large.
5. That dividend is a whole number.
6. The problem asked for the number of students altogether.
7. The difference is the number left after subtraction.
8. Count the tickets to find the total.
9. What, I wonder, is that basketball player's height?
10. He felt trapped in the tunnel's narrow width.

MEASUREMENT WORDS

Page 21: Taking Measure
1. temperature
2. distance
3. length
4. interval
5. volume

Page 22: Great Lengths
Possible answers:
1. paper; fish
2. table; sofa
3. football field; outdoor track
4. distance to school; length of trail
5. race; height of mountain

Page 23: Long-Distance Relationships
Possible answers:
1. A yard and a meter are both used to measure similar lengths. A yard equals 36 inches, and a meter is about 39.37 inches.
2. One foot equals 12 inches. They are both English units.
3. A mile is a measurement of distance between two points.
4. Length express the distance from one end of an object to the other. Interval also expresses distance, but measures the space of time between events.
5. Temperature measures heat energy in degrees. The temperature of an object affects its volume, as cold objects shrink and hot ones expand.

Page 24: More Than a Measurement?
Possible answers:
1. length of time
2. loudness
3. to put space between
4. to move slowly
5. the grounds around a house; an enclosed area for animals
6. a gauge for measuring

ENGLISH AND METRIC MEASUREMENT

Page 25: Fill It Up!
1. cup, quart, gallon
2. cup
3. pint, quart, gallon
4. gallon, liter
5. cup
6. gallons, liters

Page 26: Weighty Words
Possible answers:
1. medicine; liquid
2. coffee; sugar
3. coal; steel
4. snowflake; raindrop

Page 27: How Much Is Enough?
1. liter
2. weight
3. cup
4. gram
5. quart
6. pound
7. gallon
8. ton
9. pint
10. ounce

Page 28: What a Mess!
1. gallon; d
2. quart; j
3. cup; i
4. gram; g
5. ounce; h
6. pound; a
7. ton; b
8. liter; f
9. pint; e
10. weight; c

Pages 29–30: Unit 1 Review
A. 1. A simile is a comparison using *like* or *as*.
   2. Answers will vary.
B. 1. b; The other words are about words.
   2. d; The other words are all branches of science, and the word *science* is general.
   3. a; The other words are about numbers.
   4. d; The other words are all metric measurements.
   5. d; The other words name types of writing.
C. *Sample sentences:*
   1. Our school's janitor keeps our school spotless.
   2. The product of five and six is 30.
   3. We have to be careful when we do experiments in chemistry.
   4. Diane bought one pound of candy at the fair.
   5. We have to follow the outline before we write the story.
   6. The play was performed in the auditorium.
   7. The volume of the jug was one gallon.
   8. Very is an adverb that is often used to describe other adverbs.
   9. The library is closed on the holiday.
   10. In studying history, we learn about the past.
D. Wording will vary.
   1. to study and investigate in order to discover and explain new knowledge
   2. a person who gives or offers help or services without being paid
   3. a space of time between events or states
   4. the number resulting from dividing one number by another
   5. the number divided by another number

UNIT 2

PEOPLE IN OUR LIVES

Page 31: Everyday People
Answers will vary.

Page 32: Family Members
Sample sentences:
1. A parent molds the life of a child, which is important.
2. My aunt visits from California during holidays.
3. His uncle is teaching him to play cribbage.
4. Grandmother spends time playing the piano.
5. My grandfather tries to spoil my baby sister.

Page 33: People Puzzle

Page 34: Tell Me About It!
Paragraphs will vary.

BODY WORDS

Page 35: Verb Movement
1. twitch
2. sniff
3. blink
4. faint
5. swallow

Page 36: Body Language
1. swelling
2. Sweat
3. Thirst
4. fever
5. hunger

Page 37: Crossed Signals

Page 38: So Many Symptoms!
1. sweat
2. faint
3. twitch
4. hunger
5. swelling
6. swallow
7. fever
8. sniff
9. blink
10. thirst

PARTS OF THE BODY

Page 39: Where Will They Take You?
1. calf
2. ankle
3. kneecap
4. shin
5. tendon

Page 40: Anatomy Lesson
1. chest
2. organ
3. skull
4. forehead
5. limb

Page 41: More Anatomy
1. forehead
2. skull
3. chest
4. limb
5. organ
6. tendon
7. kneecap
8. calf
9. shin
10. ankle

Page 42: Parts of a Whole
1. ankle
2. limb
3. organ
4. tendon
5. skull
6. kneecap
7. chest
8. calf
9. forehead
10. shin

HYGIENE WORDS

Page 43: Clean and Healthy
Sample sentences:
1. Everyone should bathe daily for good health.
2. We will use the tweezers to remove the splinter and then disinfect the wound.
3. The doctor will dress the cut after she stitches it up.
4. The wound from the bite needs to have a bandage applied to it.
5. We need to follow good hygiene rules, such as keeping clean.

Page 44: Clean Up Your Act!
1. gargle
2. deodorant
3. floss
4. groom
5. lather

Page 45: Squeaky Clean

1. to pass dental thread through the teeth
2. to swirl liquid around the mouth and throat
3. foam
4. a product that masks or destroys bad odors
5. to make neat and attractive
6. actions that lead to good health
7. to wash
8. to destroy germs
9. to apply medicine and a bandage to an injured body part
10. a strip of cloth used to bind wounds

```
H E M O U T H L U L L A N D A
B Y F C L E A N S P I C A N D
S P A N S P O T L E S S F I L
M A C U L A T E B P U R L E P
E R D E O D O R A N T F O C T
A N T I D B A C T E R I S A L
H A N D R W A S H I N G S O A
P I N A E P U M E P B O T T L
E O R I S B A N D A G E N A B
A R O R S P E R H G R O O M A
P H Y G I E N E C S S O M E K
N D G A R G L E L A T H E R F
P E R D F U E M E T D N S C E
C A T N D S L E T A R E A B I
D I S I N F E C T I O N O F T
```

Page 46: Rise and Shine

Paragraphs will vary.

CHARACTER WORDS

Page 47: Who Are You?

1. appearance
2. attitude
3. behavior
4. nature
5. character

Page 48: How Others See Us

1. dislike
2. proud
3. disappointed
4. approve
5. admire

Page 49: Working Together

Sample sentences:

1. I admire the character of people who build Habitat for Humanity homes.
2. It is easy to dislike a person's bad attitude.
3. It is his nature to approve of everyone.
4. Dan was proud of his children's behavior at the fair.
5. She was disappointed when the face cream did not improve her appearance.
6. to be disappointed in someone or something

Page 50: Progress Report

Reports will vary.

READING AND BUSINESS WORDS

Page 51: Something to Read

1. catalog
2. article
3. chapter
4. magazine
5. newspaper

Page 52: Tools of the Trade

1. agenda
2. keyboard
3. network
4. tote
5. calculator

Page 53: Match 'Em

1. e 2. c 3. h 4. a 5. g 6. d 7. f 8. i 9. j 10. b

Page 54: Working Words

1. a paper printed and sold (with news) daily or weekly
2. a system of computers connected by communication lines
3. a weekly or monthly publication with pictures and articles
4. keys that print letters when pressed
5. a list of names, titles, or objects arranged in an order, often published for sale
6. a list or an outline of things to be done
7. nonfiction writing that may be in a magazine or newspaper
8. a device for doing math
9. a main division of a book or story
10. a large carrying bag

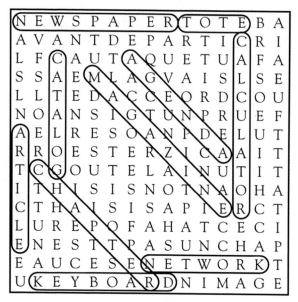

REASONS FOR LEARNING

Page 55: Light Reading
Possible answers:

1. You would read a receipt when you purchase something to see if it is correct.
2. You would read a manual for a new appliance to see if you were operating it correctly.
3. You would read a cookbook if you were preparing a meal and want to know the correct ingredients.
4. You would read an invitation to find out what the event is, where it is, and the date and time.
5. You would read correspondence to see who it is from and why it is sent to you.

Page 56: Hard Work = Benefits
Sample sentences:

1. Acceptance by one's peers is important to a teenager.
2. If you graduate from college, there will be more positions open to you.
3. Put a lot of effort into your work, and you will have more options.
4. Ellie showed respect for authority and received many compliments.
5. Work hard, and you will receive a reward.

Page 57: Look and Learn

1. compliment; expression of praise
2. manual; a book that tells how to use something
3. acceptance; state of being found worthy
4. receipt; a document noting money received
5. invitation; a written note to come to an event
6. position; a job
7. reward; something offered for special service
8. correspondence; letters
9. cookbook; a book of recipes and directions
10. options; choices

Page 58: It's All About You!
Sentences will vary.

Pages 59–60: Unit 2 Review

A. 1. c; The other words are positive.
    2. c; The other words name parts of the leg.
    3. d; The other words are body movements.
    4. c; The other words are about keeping clean.
    5. d; The other words are internal qualities.

B. 1. d
    2. c
    3. a
    4. b
    5. e

C. Wording will vary.
    1. a printed document noting money received
    2. a system of computers connected by communication lines
    3. letters
    4. something given or offered in return for special service
    5. possibilities; choices

D. *Sample sentences:*
    1. Julie received an invitation to a wedding.
    2. He was proud to be an American.
    3. Al's behavior was unreasonable and outrageous.
    4. Donna had a high fever and had to stay in bed.
    5. I dislike the way he spoke to me.
    6. He lost a limb in battle.
    7. Her good nature made her a happy person.
    8. Jacob was my partner in doing the chemistry experiment.
    9. The nurse will dress the wound from the fall.
    10. He liked his new position as an attorney.

UNIT 3

COMPARING TASTES

Page 61: Sense of Taste
Possible answers:

1. pretzels; potato chips
2. cake; syrup
3. coffee; spinach
4. lemon; lime
5. pizza; ice cream

Sentences will vary.

Page 62: Let's Compare
Sample sentences:

1. My ideas are similar to yours.
2. A dog is unlike a cat.
3. What are the differences between you and your brother?

4. Be sure to vary your sentences when you write.
5. Not all twins have identical appearances.

Page 63: Similar Tastes

1. tasting like salt
2. having qualities in common
3. tasting like sugar
4. different
5. sharp, biting taste
6. what makes two or more things not the same
7. having an acid or a spoiled taste
8. to differ
9. giving great pleasure, especially to taste or smell
10. exactly alike

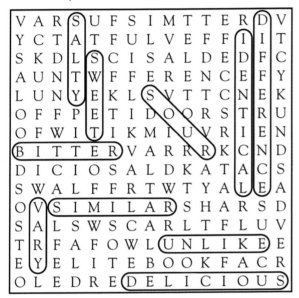

Page 64: Taste and Compare

1. vary
2. similar
3. salty
4. delicious
5. unlike
6. sour
7. identical
8. bitter
9. differences
10. sweet

MOVEMENT WORDS

Page 65: Move It!

1. bounce
2. stationary
3. crawled
4. sliding
5. tumble

Page 66: Moving Pictures

1. flipped
2. jog
3. raced
4. sprint
5. gallop

Possible synonyms:

6. turned
7. ran
8. unchanged
9. topple
10. slipping

Page 67: Moving Word Pairs

Possible answers:

1. stationary—not moving
   crawled—moving slowly
2. tumble—fall, rolling and turning
   bounce—spring back or up after hitting a surface
3. sprint—run at top speed
   raced—went at top speed
4. jog—run at an easy pace
   gallop—run in a fast manner
5. flipped—turned end over end
   sliding—moving smoothly over a surface

Page 68: Amazing Race

Letters will vary.

DESCRIBING WORDS

Page 69: Not-so-Straight

Sample sentences:

1. June's hair is curly, especially in damp weather.
2. We worked to install the shelf, but it is still in crooked.
3. The driveway to the estate curved to the front door.
4. The holiday decorations formed a spiral of many colors.
5. A lighthouse is an interesting circular building.

Page 70: How Does It Look?

Possible answers:

1. clothes; sunset
2. weather; notion
3. speed; sight
4. grades; story
5. yard; house

Sentences will vary.

Page 71: Choose a Letter!

1. d 2. h 3. f 4. b 5. i 6. a 7. e 8. g 9. j 10. c

Page 72: Crossroads

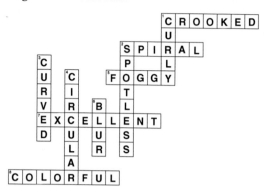

OUR SENSES

Page 73: How Does It Feel?
1. softest
2. firm
3. roughest
4. coarse
5. tender

Sample antonyms:
6. tough
7. smooth
8. soft
9. roughest
10. softest

Page 74: Ouch and Yuck!
1. bumpy
2. slippery
3. sticky
4. jagged
5. squishy
Sentences will vary.

Page 75: Touchy Adjectives
Possible answers:
1. ground; handshake
2. skin; velvet
3. hair; cloth
4. meat; care
5. boards; sandpaper
6. glass; saw
7. road; walkway
8. candy; molasses
9. marsh; seaweed
10. ice; roads

Page 76: Pair 'Em Up!
Sample sentences:
1. I like a couch that is not too firm.
2. This flannel shirt is the softest one I own.
3. The surface of the walk was coarse and rough.
4. The bruise I received when I fell is still tender.
5. This tissue is the roughest paper I've ever used!
6. I was cut by the jagged glass of the broken window.
7. I rode my bicycle on a very bumpy road.
8. The spilled syrup made the table very sticky.
9. My shoes got dirty in the squishy mud.
10. The outside stairs were slippery from the ice.

DEGREE WORDS

Page 77: To What Degree?
Sample sentences:
1. The cider had a mild taste.
2. My ability is moderate when it comes to sports.
3. New England often has severe weather in the winter.
4. We solved a minor issue dealing with curfew.
5. Drunk driving is a major problem.

Page 78: Speedy Words
Sample sentences:
1. We need to accelerate as we drive up the mountain.
2. A turtle is one of the slowest animals.
3. The highway is the quickest way to the mall.
4. He is a swift runner.
5. The flood waters are very rapid under the bridge.

Page 79: A Little Shuffle
1. rapid; very fast
2. severe; very strict or harsh
3. mild; gentle
4. slowest; moving at a speed less than the rest
5. major; great in number or performance
6. swift; moving with great speed
7. accelerate; to increase speed
8. quickest; fastest
9. minor; small in size or importance
10. moderate; neither very good nor bad

Page 80: A Big Problem
Letters will vary.

TIME WORDS

Page 81: When?
1. recent
2. afterward
3. earlier
4. previous
5. sooner

Page 82: How Often?
Sample sentences:
1. Jill usually arrives at school early.
2. Luis likes an occasional ice cream.
3. You can build up frequent flyer miles if you travel a lot.
4. Rarely do we see an eagle.
5. We seldom go to a play.

Page 83: A Puzzling Time

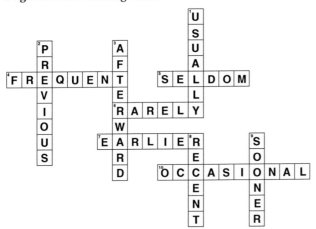

Page 84: Time Difference
Possible answers:
1. sooner—earlier than expected
   previous—time before
2. earlier—before today
   afterward—later than sometime
3. recent—happening a short time ago
   frequent—happening often
4. occasional—happening infrequently
   rarely—hardly ever happening
5. seldom—not often
   usually—happening most of the time

ADJECTIVES AND VERBS

Page 85: How Did It Happen?
1. uneven
2. dramatic
3. gradual
4. somewhat
5. barely

Page 86: Changes
Sample sentences:
1. The radio is too loud so we need to adjust the volume.
2. The dress was too long so we will modify the length so it will fit.
3. There is an increase in the number of soccer games.
4. The class would like a decrease in homework over the vacation week.
5. We can maintain good health by eating properly and exercising.

Page 87: Sound Check
Sentences will vary.

Page 88: Pairing Up!
1. c 2. e 3. g 4. a 5. h 6. i 7. b 8. j 9. f 10. d

Pages 89–90: Unit 3 Review
A. 1. A synonym is a word that means almost the same thing as another word.
   2. An antonym is a word that means the opposite of another word.
B. 1. c; The other words are about something happening before something else.
   2. a; The other words are about things that are not the same.
   3. a; The other words are about raised textures.
   4. b; The other words are about movement.
   5. c; The other words are all extreme words that end in -est (superlatives).
C. *Possible answers:*
   1. outstanding; inferior
   2. fast; slow
   3. small; greater
   4. change; retain
   5. enlarge; decrease
D. *Sample sentences:*
   1. Studying will accelerate your progress in the subject.
   2. Mike seldom forgets to call his friends.
   3. A hot stove can cause severe burns.
   4. Daily exercise helps one maintain physical fitness.
   5. When the weather warms up, we will see a gradual melting of snow.

UNIT 4

FUN WORDS

Page 91: Good Times
Sample sentences:
1. The cheer of the excited crowd gave the football players more energy.
2. It is a thrill to ride a roller coaster.
3. Our vacation to Hawaii was enjoyable.
4. The daily comics are fun to read and humorous.
5. We had good weather on our trip, which made the days pleasurable.

Page 92: Party Time!
1. jokes
2. surprise
3. circus
4. celebration
5. carnival

Page 93: Clowning Around
Letters will vary.

Page 94: All Mixed-Up
1. circus; a traveling show with acrobats, jugglers, wild animals, and so forth
2. excited; having stirred up feelings

3. carnival; a festival, with rides and games
4. jokes; short stories with funny endings
5. pleasurable; agreeable
6. thrill; a sudden feeling of excitement
7. surprise; something that comes without warning
8. enjoyable; being a source of pleasure
9. celebration; a festive gathering to mark a special event
10. humorous; funny

SAD WORDS

Page 95: Sad Times
Possible answers:

1. not invited to a party; being left alone
2. not telling the truth; not helping at home
3. over a test; over being late for school
4. after seeing a movie; of being lost in the woods
5. at a friend for not calling; at not being able to go to a game

Page 96: A Painful Part

1. loss
2. sadness
3. injury
4. sickness
5. distress

Page 97: Painful Puzzel

Page 98: Pairing Off
Sample sentences:

1. The older man was lonely.
2. Wrong actions often lead to guilty feelings.
3. Mother was worried when we were not home on time.
4. The young child was scared of the clown.
5. The child began feeling angry after her balloon burst.
6. Fever is a common symptom of sickness.
7. Injuries in sports such as football are common.
8. Distress and depression may send a person to the hospital.

9. The child experienced feelings of loss when she found her toy box empty.
10. Relatives of the deceased shed tears of sadness at the funeral.

NICE AND NOT-SO-NICE WORDS

Page 99: Be Nice!
Sentences will vary.

Page 100: Not-so-Nice
1. selfish
2. greedy
3. Teasing
4. unfair
5. cruel

Page 101: Help or Harm?

Page 102: Looking for Help
1. giving aid to someone
2. taking care of oneself only
3. having concern for another
4. ready to hurt others
5. free in giving
6. not fair or honest
7. honest
8. making fun of
9. showing pity for another
10. trying to grab more than one's share

```
C I N G Y T E A S I N G R A T
H E L P F U L A I L M E N H S
U R C L E Z G U N F A I R E R
G E N A E C O M C E I J G L E
R E S P R I N G E E A T E P E
E R N A I I S S R O M Y C J F
E S P E C P N E E O U S R U D
D Y E W R L S G D I N G U L L
Y G O L L O S E C S P R E P Y
I N G T F I U E N S A T L E G
L T A T E I S L Y T O U S O
C A T N F I S H T U E L C O N
G R R A N D A H N O U S R G X
D G P T R Y R A N F T F A R Y
C O M P A S S I O N A T E R E
```

BEHAVIOR WORDS

Page 103: Words Behaving Badly
1. Cheating
2. harm
3. dishonest
4. disrespect
5. stealing

Page 104: Staying Safe
1. rule
2. boundary
3. limit
4. shun
5. obey

Page 105: Wisdom of the Ages
Explanations will vary.

Page 106: Your Own World
Rules will vary.

COMMUNICATION AND INTERACTION

Page 107: Let's Talk
1. complain
2. respond
3. ignore
4. agree
5. discuss

Page 108: Talk It Out
Sample sentences:
1. Books help to educate readers.
2. Please assist those who need help.
3. When we demonstrate erosion, students learn better than if they just read about it.

4. I suggest you put more effort into your studying.
5. Listening to a patient's complaints helps doctors and nurses provide the proper care.

Page 109: Some Good Advice
Letters will vary.

Page 110: And the Letter Is...
1. d 2. i 3. g 4. a 5. j 6. h 7. c 8. f 9. b 10. e

VISION WORDS

Page 111: Look and See
Sample sentences:
1. It is not polite to stare at people.
2. I had to peek into the closet to see what I was getting for my birthday.
3. I love to gaze at a full moon.
4. Please help me search for my pencil.
5. One glance at my report card and I knew my parents would be pleased.

Page 112: Seeing Is Believing
Possible answers:
1. stars; sunrise
2. book; video
3. birds; mountain
4. moon; stars
5. movie; exercise program

Page 113: A Starting Point
1. telescope
2. stare
3. video, vision
4. search

Page 114: Looking Good
1. c 2. g 3. e 4. f 5. j 6. i 7. h 8. b 9. a 10. d

TENSE WORDS

Page 115: All Shook Up!
Possible answers:
1. impatient; uninterested
2. uneasy; relieved
3. unsure; certain
4. undecided; positive
5. excitable; calm
Sentences will vary.

Page 116: Scary Vocabulary!
Sample sentences:
1. The frightened child was found near the lake.
2. I felt horror at the sight of the accident.
3. We heard a terrified scream as we started down the path.

4. Sue feels panic when it is dark.

5. The girls were fearful of the shadows of the trees.

Page 117: Worry Words

Page 118: Worried or Scared?

Possible answers:

1. panic—overwhelming fear

   horror—dread or shock

2. nervous—easily excited

   frightened—very afraid or alarmed

3. fearful—expecting something bad to happen

   doubtful—not certain of outcome

4. terrified—extremely afraid

   anxious—afraid of what may happen

5. uncertain—unsure

   eager—desiring very much or impatient

Sentences will vary.

Pages 119–120: Unit 4 Review

A. 1. d; The other words are about bad behavior.

   2. b; The other words are about fear.

   3. d; The other words are about helping.

   4. d; All the words are about seeing, but vision (d) is the only word that is not a tool for seeing.

   5. d; The other words are about fun.

B. *Sample synonyms:*

   1. frightened

   2. unsure

   3. thrilled

   4. funny

   5. illness

C. 1. sure

   2. happiness

   3. fair

   4. dishonest

   5. painful

D. 1. b

   2. a

   3. e

4. d

5. c

UNIT 5

TRANSPORTATION WORDS

Page 121: Transportation Time

Sample sentences:

1. A bus is a vehicle.

2. Jim's automobile was very old and rusty.

3. The taxi will pick us up early and take us to the airport.

4. Dave rides a motorcycle to work.

5. Amy rides her scooter in the parking lot.

Page 122: Carrier Choices

1. ski lift

2. space shuttle

3. rocket

4. airline

5. helicopter

Page 123: Any Letters for Me?

1. taxi

2. airline

3. ski lift

4. scooter

5. automobile

6. space shuttle

7. helicopter

8. motorcycle

9. rocket

10. vehicle

Page 124: Wish You Were Here!

Letters will vary.

MORE TRANSPORTATION WORDS

Page 125: One if by Land

1. tricycle

2. horseback

3. carriage

4. wagon

5. bicycle

Page 126: Two if by Sea

Sample sentences:

1. The motorboat shot over the waves.

2. A yacht is a luxury ship.

3. The submarine was loaded with torpedoes before going into battle.

4. Riding a surfboard in ocean waves is thrilling.

5. A rowboat is a good craft to fish from.

Page 127: Mixed-Up Travel

1. surfboard; long narrow board that floats; used in surfing

2. wagon; vehicle with four wheels, no motor; used to carry goods

3. horseback; on the back of a horse

4. yacht; small ship used for pleasure

5. motorboat; small boat driven by gas or electric motor

6. tricycle; vehicle with three wheels moved by pedals

7. rowboat; a boat rowed with oars

8. submarine; naval ship that operates underwater

9. bicycle; vehicle with two wheels, one behind the other; moved by pedals

10. carriage; vehicle with wheels, no motor, that carries people

Page 128: By Land or by Sea?

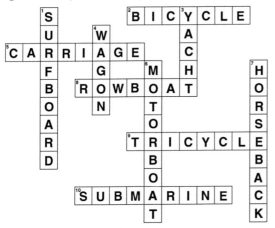

WEATHER WORDS

Page 129: Water, Water Everywhere

1. rainwater

2. humid

3. moisture

4. drench

5. flooded

Page 130: You're All Wet

Sample sentences:

1. Better bring your umbrella because the forecast is for rain.

2. My raincoat keeps me dry in storms.

3. The forecast is for sunny weather.

4. Dad has to replace the worn wipers on his car.

5. Paper towels are great for wiping up spills.

Page 131: Mopping Up with Metaphors

Metaphors will vary.

Page 132: Weather on the Way!

Forecasts will vary.

MORE WEATHER WORDS

Page 133: Brrr . . .

Answers will vary.

Page 134: Storm Front

Sample sentences:

1. A warm summer breeze helps me relax.

2. Weather forecasters warn of the danger of hurricanes.

3. The siren sounded a tornado warning.

4. The gale might tumble the tree in our front yard.

5. The cold sleet is making my fingers numb.

Page 135: Puzzling Weather

1. a long, heavy snowstorm

2. a gentle wind

3. freezing cold

4. a covering of tiny ice crystals on a cold surface

5. a strong wind

6. small lumps of ice that fall from clouds, sometimes in a thunderstorm

7. a tropical cyclone

8. frozen or partly frozen rain

9. covered with snow

10. a violent whirling wind shaped like a funnel.

```
E S N O W Y E Z O W S I F F T
A S H E B R E E Z E S L E E T
G T U C H O W A R H E R S H D
G A R A L E C O N E C O L E S
S I R T I N G I R L T I L E Z
T O I A R Y Z A L E Y O S T Z
Z Z C T O P S B L I Z Z A R D
H E A G O T C K E C H R S T
I L N R C K N M F I A F F R D
R R E H U R Z Z F R Y Q R Z U
F R I G I D T O R N A D O R M
D Y Z H C K S T N M A Z S Y A
K A V N H A I L M A T E T R I
Z R I N G A R D S T A R T E R
O R A R D A B E C I D O E U Y
```

Page 136: Which Weather?

1. e 2. a 3. g 4. c 5. h 6. i 7. f 8. b 9. j 10. d

PROBLEM WORDS

Page 137: We Have a Problem!

Sample sentences:

1. That disease can be treated with antibiotics.

2. The boy on the sled had an accident when the sled flew off the slope.

3. Try to make more friends than enemies.

4. Try not to embarrass friends by telling stories about them.

5. The cat's litter box has an unpleasant odor.

Page 138: Something Gone Bad

Sample sentences:

1. The building was ruined by the fire.

2. I made only one error in my homework.

3. Milk will spoil if not refrigerated.
4. Your bike will rust in this rain.
5. Sorry I'm late for dinner, but my computer malfunctioned and had to be fixed.

Page 139: Poor Rusty
Stories will vary.

Page 140: Looking for Trouble
1. an illness or change that keeps a living thing from functioning normally
2. damaged beyond repair
3. something bad that happens by chance
4. a mistake
5. people who hate, attack, or try to harm someone
6. to decay
7. to cause to feel uncomfortable
8. reddish coating on metal when exposed to moist air
9. a smell
10. a failure to work properly

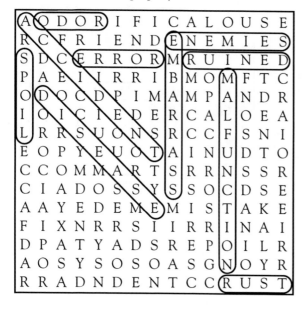

PROBLEM SOLVING

Page 141: Fix It Up!
Sample sentences:
1. I hope to repair my broken fishing rod.
2. You should offer to replace the dish you broke.
3. When you make a mistake, you should correct it.
4. Have you found the solution to problem 3 yet?
5. During California's gold rush, thousands of common people hoped to discover gold and get rich.

Page 142: Make Your Case
1. logic
2. persist
3. confirm
4. rational
5. reason

Page 143: Solving Words
Possible answers:
1. repair—to fix; replace—to put something new in its place
2. discover—to find; persist—to continue stubbornly
3. confirm—to prove by facts; rational—reasonable, showing understanding
4. solution—the answer; correct—to make right
5. reason—intelliegence; logic—sound reasoning, common sense

Page 144: Fixer-Upper

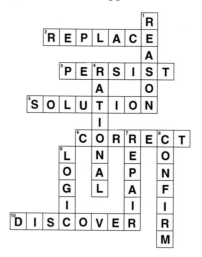

TEACHING AND LEARNING

Page 145: Constructive Work
1. scholar
2. advice
3. practice
4. desire
5. instruction

Page 146: Levels of Learning
Sample sentences:
1. The plumber is capable of doing that task.
2. It was clumsy of me to break the chair.
3. When one is skillful, it is easy to do many things.
4. In time, you will be experienced in whatever you study.
5. If I master this computer game, I can get to the next level.

Page 147: Sentence Completions
Sentences will vary.

Page 148: Puzzle Practice

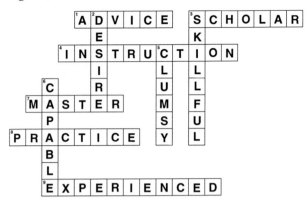

Pages 149–150: Unit 5 Review

A. 1. b; The other words name vehicles with wheels, land transportation vehicles, and vehicles without engines.
2. d; The other words name water transportation.
3. d; The other words are about thinking or the mind.
4. b; The other words are about water.
5. a; The other words are about wind.

B. Wording will vary.
1. a failure to work properly
2. to continue stubbornly
3. to become very skilled at something
4. to remove doubt by giving facts
5. to put something new in the place of something else

C. 1. b
2. e
3. a
4. d
5. c

D. *Sample sentences:*
1. The vehicle was stolen from the parking garage.
2. You can discover antiques at a flea market.
3. The food will spoil if left in the sun.
4. A severe blizzard can leave a city helpless.
5. The surgeon was skillful in attaching the limb.

E. 1. fix
2. cold
3. damp
4. soak
5. sickness

UNIT 6
BANKING AND EATING WORDS

Page 151: Bank On It!
Sample sentences:
1. This is the week I deposit my allowance money.
2. My mom will have to withdraw money to make a payment on her mortgage.
3. I have a bank account in my own name.
4. Many people use a checking account to pay their bills.
5. Marie started a savings account to finance her future college expenses.

Page 152: Out to Lunch
1. reserve
2. serve
3. prepare
4. order
5. deliver

Page 153: Food Bank
1. prepare
2. account
3. deposit
4. deliver
5. order
6. savings
7. reserve
8. withdraw
9. serve
10. checking

Page 154: Relating Words
Sample sentences:
1. I will deposit money in my account.
2. Peter has both a savings and a checking account.
3. The waiter served our order.
4. You must withdraw money from the bank to pay the workers who will deliver the furniture.
5. Better prepare to go out to eat, while I reserve a table for us.

SHOPPING AND EATING WORDS

Page 155: Out to Eat
Possible answers:
1. rolls; cake
2. sandwich; coffee
3. casseroles; soup
4. salads; sliced ham
5. bacon and eggs; apple pie
Sentences will vary.

Page 156: Shopping for Words
Sample sentences:
1. The wheels on my shopping cart are not working right.
2. This store carries low-priced merchandise.
3. I received a five-percent discount at that store by using their card.
4. At three for a dollar, that's a very good value.
5. What a variety of fruits that grocery store carries!

Page 157: Shop Around
1. f 2. d 3. h 4. b. 5. g 6. c 7. i 8. j 9. a 10. e

Page 158: Cheap Eats

SHOPPING AND WORKING WORDS

Page 159: What's Your Role?

1. cashier
2. salesperson
3. security
4. customer
5. custodian

Page 160: Shopping List
Sample sentences:

1. I always select ripe fruit.
2. The customer received a refund for the broken appliance.
3. The blanket was my best purchase.
4. He bargaineed and got a great deal on a used car.
5. When using a new medicine, be sure to read the information on the label.

Page 161: Looking for a Bargain

1. a person who sells something in a store or door-to-door
2. to choose
3. people who ensure safety
4. to give back or repay
5. a person who buys from a store or company
6. to buy
7. a person who cleans a certain place
8. to discuss the terms of a purchase
9. a person who runs a store's register
10. to attach a paper to something to identify it or describe it

```
B P U R P E T L I F E L O S S
A F U N D Y S E L E C T D E I
Y I M A C U S T O D I A N A T
O S A L T R A I R T E A R A T
F O U L B A L L C U S T O M E R
D B R E Y F E U C H N B F C H
P U R C H A S E S G L G U Y L
C L H E C K P I E E A A T G R
G F Y C F S E A C A S E B Y I
C A S H I E R D U F D U N E T
C B I S G C S U R I T U M B L
B Y L A K E O F I R E F U N D
A D R I E R N Y T S E L E S T
B A R G A I N A Y C H P E R S
B O G R X F U N D A I N S O N
```

Page 162: Suggestion Box
Letters will vary.

BUSINESS WORDS

Page 163: Down to Business
Sample sentences:

1. I will agree to that transaction.
2. A tree service is what we need.
3. The club employs a lifeguard for the summer season.
4. Tyrone's salary will increase next year.
5. I worked ten hours of overtime last week.

Page 164: Doing Business

1. Competition
2. schedule
3. billing
4. delivery
5. damaged

Page 165: Business Partners
Sample sentences:

1. The boss made out a schedule for overtime.
2. There is much competition for that service.
3. The transaction will be complete with the delivery of the goods.
4. Some companies employ workers on an hourly basis, while others pay a salary.
5. The billing had to be adjusted because of the damaged goods.

Page 166: Business Terms
Definitions will vary.

1. a business deal
2. to hire for pay or salary
3. time spent working that is more than one usually works

4. a contest
5. transfer of goods
6. work or action that is useful to others
7. a set amount of money paid for work done
8. harmed
9. a list of times
10. recording goods sold and asking for the money owed for them

BENEFIT WORDS

Page 167: To Your Benefit!
Possible answers:
1. A promotion is often given to hard-working employees.
2. Those who work hard will have a brighter future.
3. Friendships take effort but are very rewarding.
4. If you work hard at something, you can gain expertise in that area.
5. Those who make an effort to contribute to the success of a business are admired and respected.

Page 168: Great Results
1. selection
2. respect
3. vacations
4. luxury
5. housing

Page 169: Goals for Myself
Sentences will vary.

Page 170: Priorities
Paragraphs will vary.

GOVERNMENT AND TRAVEL

Page 171: In Office
Sample sentences:
1. The mayor rode in the Veterans' Day parade.
2. Our governor is in conference with a group of mayors.
3. He was elected a senator and went to Washington, D.C.
4. The American people elect their representatives.
5. The fire commissioner oversees the alarms and sprinklers of public buildings.

Page 172: Passing Through
Answers will vary.

Page 173: Who Is Who?
1. d 2. a 3. g 4. j 5. b 6. e 7. i 8. h 9. f 10. c

Page 174: Where's the Leader?

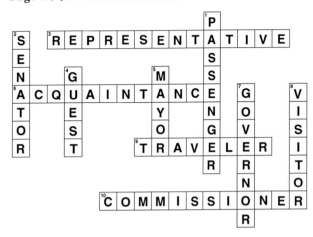

JOURNEYS AND EXPLORATION

Page 175: Miles to Go
Possible answers:
1. take a sea voyage; join an expedition to Africa
2. travel with a musical group; a sightseeing trip
3. investigate a cave; travel into an unknown place
4. early settler in the West; frontiersman like Davy Crockett
5. cattle on the plains; rove through the fields
Sentences will vary.

Page 176: Travel Time
Sample sentences:
1. We can learn much from studying the past.
2. They saw ancient artifacts in the museum.
3. A brave knight was usually rewarded well.
4. The pyramid was an awesome sight, built with enormous stone.
5. We were told never to disturb a sacred tomb.

Page 177: Seeing the Sites
Letters will vary.

Page 178: Where Were We?
1. pyramid; a large stone structure built in Egypt
2. past; time gone by
3. pioneer; an early settler
4. tour; a trip that ends where it starts and shows people things along the way
5. knight; a medieval warrior
6. tomb; a grave for dead people
7. explore; to go into to find something new
8. journey; a long trip
9. roam; to go from place to place with no real purpose or direction
10. museum; a building that displays objects of interest

Pages 179–180: Unit 6 Review

A. 1. c; The other words are about money.

2. c; The other words are about traveling.

3. a; The other words name elected officials.

4. b: The other words name places.

5. a; The other words are about money.

B. *Sample sentences:*

1. Rosie is the cashier at the hospital's cafeteria.

2. There is a variety of merchandise in a department store.

3. The pioneer set out to explore the mountains.

4. When I receive a promotion, I will be able to put more money into my savings account.

5. Taking Caribbean vacations is a luxury.

C. 1. expertise

2. respect

3. tour

4. custodian

5. schedule

D. Wording will vary.

1. a restaurant where people serve themselves

2. a place to live for a number of people

3. someone riding on or in a vehicle

4. to discuss the terms of a purchase or an agreement

5. to buy

Share Your Bright Ideas

We want to hear from you!

Your name_____Date_____

School name_____

School address_____

City _____State _____Zip_____Phone number (_____)_____

Grade level(s) taught_____Subject area(s) taught_____

Where did you purchase this publication?_____

In what month do you purchase a majority of your supplements?_____

What moneys were used to purchase this product?

____School supplemental budget   ____Federal/state funding   ____Personal

Please "grade" this Walch publication in the following areas:

Quality of service you received when purchasing .... A   B   C   D

Ease of use.. A   B   C   D

Quality of content.. A   B   C   D

Page layout .... A   B   C   D

Organization of material .... A   B   C   D

Suitability for grade level... A   B   C   D

Instructional value... A   B   C   D

COMMENTS:_____

_____

What specific supplemental materials would help you meet your current—or future—instructional needs?

_____

Have you used other Walch publications? If so, which ones?_____

May we use your comments in upcoming communications?   ____Yes   ____No

Please **FAX** this completed form to **888-991-5755**, or mail it to

Customer Service, J. Weston Walch, Publisher, P. O. Box 658, Portland, ME 04104-0658

We will send you a **FREE GIFT** in appreciation of your feedback. **THANK YOU!**